Motivated by Wicked Intention

A True Story of Demonic Oppression
Caused by Witchcraft in a Small Town.

CAROL BELL

MOTIVATED BY WICKED INTENTION
A True Story of Demonic Oppression Caused by Witchcraft in a Small Town.

Copyright © 2017, 2020 Carol Bell.

All rights reserved. No part of this book may be used or reproduced by any means, graphic, electronic, or mechanical, including photocopying, recording, taping or by any information storage retrieval system without the written permission of the author except in the case of brief quotations embodied in critical articles and reviews.

The NIV text may be quoted in any form (written, visual, electronic, or audio), up to and inclusive of one thousand (1,000) verses without express written permission of the publisher, providing the verses quoted do not amount to a complete book of the total text of the work in which they are quoted.

Scripture taken from the Holy Bible, New International Version. Copyright 1993, 1978, and 1984 by International Bible Society. Used by permission of Zondervan Publishing House.

The Copy Collective Press books may be ordered through booksellers or by contacting:

The Copy Collective Press
416 Marion Oaks
Ocala, FL 34473
www.thecopycollectivepresscom
1-775-468-3761

Because of the dynamic nature of the Internet, any web addresses or links contained in this book may have changed since publication and may no longer be valid. The views expressed in this work are solely those of the author and do not necessarily reflect the views of the publisher, and the publisher hereby disclaims any responsibility for them.

Any people depicted in stock imagery provided by Pixabay are models, and such images are being used for illustrative purposes only. © pixabay

First Edition's ISBN (Softcover): 978-1-5320-2730-7
First Edition's ISBN (Hardcover): 978-1-5320-2732-1
First Edition's ISBN (eBook): 978-1-5320-2731-4

Second Edition's ISBN (Softcover): 978-1-970160-13-0
Second Edition's ISBN (eBook): 978-1-970160-31-4

CONTENTS

Dedication	vii
Appreciation	ix
Preface	xi
Investigate Living Conditions	1
God and Relationships	3
Christian on the Front Line	10
Living Arrangement	21
Heartbreaking News	24
Deceived by Deception	27
Physical Effect	34
Outrageous Neighbors	38
Home Invasion by Evil Spirits	43
Life-Defining Moment	52
Dark Magic and Demonic Spirits	61
Manipulation of Energies	69
Victory over Opposition	72
Insight into Demonic Oppression and Possession	81
Forgiving Your Enemies	88
Bible Scriptures	91
Author's Biography	99

In honor of my precious daughter, Jeanine.

To my lovely daughter, who is caring, sensitive, inquisitive, and precious all in one. To your innocence, optimism, and curious need to know specific answers to things that are not so easily explained. There were many secrets hidden from you because you weren't ready to be exposed to the onset of Tristan's visitation. Your grief and despair were too intense; there was no need to add more sorrow. I wanted to keep you protected at all costs by not saying anything.

It was necessary to wait until you were strong enough to comprehend everything you are about to read. Your dad and I initiated our greatest efforts in keeping you confident, optimistic, motivated, and encouraged. Shielding you with God's love, protection, and peace was what was needed.

A mother's love means sparing her child from being afflicted by more sorrow than necessary. We're living in an era when all people need to be encouraged, knowing that circumstances change.

Certain things in life take us through hoops. How we pursue change is up to us. Even through our awkward moments, the Lord gives us the capability to overcome every hindrance, impediment, and problem. It's no accident that God chose us to be your caregivers and protectors, just as God has entrusted you with twin boys to cherish and love forever.

God will always cherish and love you eternally. God gives gifts to his children undeservingly because of his love for us.

Therefore, we're held responsible for what we do with the gift he has given. Tristan's four years of life represented love, joy, and laughter. God chose the perfect parents to be his guardians, and both should be proud of your accomplishments.

I am proud that Tristan was the life flow of our lives. Without him, our lives wouldn't have been complete God always transforms our distasteful moments. He turns them into something more meaningful, making our circumstances appear as though we have never been through anything. Daevon and the rest of my grandchildren are truly blessings sent from God's heavenly treasure.

I can finally share my entire experience. I was deliberately deceived by people practicing witchcraft. I was ensnared by demonic spirits impersonating my deceased grandson. For this reason, I would always affirm that Tristan is with God and happy. Now you can understand why I had behaved unusually and acted to protect myself.

APPRECIATION

Special thanks to my love, who is my strength, my covering, and my biggest supporter. Never have you ever left me to fend for myself. The storm was inconsiderate of our conditioning, although collectively, we both endured to the end. I am truly blessed God allows me to be your wife, and I can't imagine life without you.

I am forever appreciative to my bishop and his wife for their unconditional love and respect toward me, continually laboring in the spirit and praying for my breakthrough and deliverance. I am honored to have both of you as my spiritual parents.

To both of my aunts—Claudette and Della—I appreciate your kindness, dedication, and encouragement. Thank you for allowing God to use you as spiritual instruments on my behalf.

To my spiritual mother, Sallie, you've always loved and respected me unconditionally and listened patiently. Your heart is full of spiritual wisdom. I thank you and love you for supporting me.

To my closest friend, Nancy, I am so grateful we have reunited once again. Christ understood my need to be acquainted with someone who had similar experiences as I.

I also acknowledge my two granddaughters for helping me with my writing throughout this process, and I love them.

I can't stress enough of my appreciation of those who supported me through prayers, encouraging words, unity, and smiles. Most important, thank you for treating me with respect and dignity. My greatest gratitude comes from knowing that God looked beyond my faults and saw me.

PREFACE

Throughout the process of writing this memoir, I was exposed to a world I previously had no knowledge of. I learned about the personal and secretive lives some people have. I learned about the facades some people, even Christians, put on so that we believe they are people they truly are not. I gained knowledge of how witchcraft and the church are connected. I learned that the subject matter of witchcraft or black magic doesn't have a voice, because no one speaks on this type of issue; even if the person was plagued by such. I learned that a person that was once tainted by witchcraft does not talk about such topics. There are tons of books and videos on the subject but no one is concerned because it doesn't affect them. I view life and the world around me in a different way. Society has become irresponsible and has lost all moral and respect for mankind. I also learned that immoral behavior is not caused by our intent but rather influenced by negative thoughts and actions, which attract evil spirits. I discovered why people get angry with one another, get violent, and don't understand why. Throughout all my experiences, I became a stronger, more understanding, and less judgmental person. I now better understand what God is like and the way he works.

INVESTIGATE LIVING CONDITIONS

When we transition into a new community, we often only realize what appeals most to the eye. We are living in a time when it's necessary to be watchful and aware of our surroundings. Neighborhood watch used to be employed by concerned citizens to help safeguard against unlawful conduct. Not anymore!

We don't think about whether the area is quiet, safe, secure, or even protected. Blinded by its beautiful scenery, we do not investigate our place of residence thoroughly. Neither do we acknowledge what kinds of neighbors are living among us. Every family wants the perfect environment, where everyone living within the community is mature and responsible. But subtle, hidden danger zones are waiting for the next target.

Life, as we imagine it to be, comes with some hidden agendas. Is it because we fail to recognize there's an enemy in the camp, or is it something we prefer not to see? You usually don't expect communities to have hidden agendas. Everyone desires to live in a respectable and civilized society, free of any criminal intention. We think our communities are the safest places to live until the unexpected surfaces.

Individuals conceal their identities and deceive their friends and communities in many ways, such as dispositions, prestige, relationships, relatives, automobiles, employment, businesses, churches, leadership, acquaintances, and organizations. They are perceived as productive citizens within the community. But they camouflage their demeanor, fooling innocent individuals every day, including close relatives.

Mean-spirited people are heartless, cold, and sinful. Some may fail to realize the problems their behaviors bring to their lives and those of others. Our lives are at risk every day from the unseen forces of darkness. We can't afford to be ignorant of the enemy's wicked devices. The Bible declares, "Why do the heathen rage and the people imagine vain things?" (Psalm 2:1 KJV). The hearts of the wicked are continuously evil. We are innocent bystanders, journeying through this complex world. It's filled with plenty of violence and hatred toward our brothers and sisters. We come here vulnerable. But one thing is for sure; we can depend on God. God knows us by name and every detail of us. There are billions of people on earth, but God knows each of us personally. God is the light that shined in darkness, and the darkness has not comprehended it as of yet (John 1:5 KJV).Wickedness hides behind closed doors, hoping no one discovers the secret of evil.

GOD AND RELATIONSHIPS

All scriptures were given by inspiration and breathe out by God to set in motion guidelines for righteous living. God has implemented laws profitable for doctrine for reproof, correction, and training in righteousness. God constructed this universe based on us having a close relationship with him, recognizing who he is to us. He created us with the intention that we love and know him personally with all our hearts, souls, and minds. Christ desires to be known as Lord and reveals this with his presence to humanity. His attributes are revealed through His wisdom (Word), through his infinite (Never-ending), through his sovereignty (Supreme authority and power), God is Merciful, and God is Immutable (eternal). God has entrusted everything to his beloved son (Christ), and created the universe through Him. Christ is the radiance of His father glory and the expression of His divine nature, and sustains all things by His powerful word. God of creation is unique and divine in nature. Christ is the bridegroom, waiting to meet his bride to celebrate eternal life in the kingdom of heaven. The infinite God is not to be equal to nor compared to anyone other than himself.

The Holy Spirit is fully God He is eternal, omniscient,

omnipotent, and omnipresent. The Holy Spirit has a will and can speak to us. Too often, God and Satan are presented as fairy-tale characters. But God is not imaginary or nonexistent; the Lord is very real God the father, God the Son, and God the Holy Spirit are the three distinct personalities. Therefore God the father, the Son, and the Holy Spirit is the divine Godhead, each one has a specific mission to accomplish, to reconcile humankind to God (God: Galatians 4:4–5), (Jesus: John 6:37–38), (Holy Spirit: John 14:26, 16:8, Romans 1:19–20 NIV) (Copyright 1993, 1978, and 1984 by International Bible Society).

Who do you value more: God or the evil one? The only way a human being can form a comprehensible relationship with God is through divine revelation of himself through the Bible. The Spirit of God is distinctive, and there are no other gods besides Him (Exodus 20:3 KJV). God is light, and there is no darkness in Him. Darkness doesn't stand a chance against our Lord and Savior Jesus Christ. Light is the spirit of Gods nature and character. The Lord Himself said for the God of this world system has come, and has nothing in me (John 12:31 NKV).

God has instinctive attributes about himself. He's the all-powerful God. He's the perfect God. He's the God of all wisdom. He's the God that redeems. And he's the God of existence. Meanwhile, there is so much to understand that God is. There's nothing God won't do for his children.

God sent his only Son, Jesus, who knows no sin. Jesus bore

the sins of all humankind to reconcile humanity to right standing with God. The phrases, "In the beginning" and "From the beginning" have different meanings. "In the beginning" has to do with eternity, and "From the beginning" means as far back as human experience. God explains at the beginning of creation was the Word (Jesus), and the Word was with God, and the Word was God (John 1:1 KJV). God is the truth, the way, and the light, and no one shall enter without the approval of Lord Jesus Christ (John 14:6 KJV).

God, through the Holy Ghost, has everything to do with creation; he spoke it, and the divine Holy Ghost performs it. Life was in the Word, and the Word was the light of humankind (John 1:4 KJV). Therefore, without light affecting darkness, humankind would be susceptible to darkness rather than the light that comes from salvation. All things were created through Jesus, and apart from the Word, not one thing was created (John 1:3 KJV). Those sayings are self-explanatory.

The Lord is the originator of all creation, the source designed for our existence, and architect of the entire universe. The Holy Ghost is a respectable citizen of Christ. The Holy Spirit is the ultimate representative between humankind and God. The purpose of God's Spirit is to remind us of the revelatory teaching of Christ Jesus and to glorify his name. God created us through his Spirit as a free moral agent to choose whether to serve him. Under no circumstances does he intend to dictate our lives to us. Rather, he purposely left those decisions to our discretion (Deuteronomy 30:19, John 3:16, Matthews 7:7–8 NIV).

In this world, everything we implement, verbalize, contemplate, experience, and sermonize is spiritual in nature, spoken by his divine Spirit. Therefore, humans are spirits in human flesh to live in this physical dimension. The Spirit of God is necessary to maintain our existence. Many things in the heavens are invisible, but those who unleash the secret mysteries through their spiritual development attain knowledge. God of creation is greater than the world could ever imagine him to be. God's power is the principal guiding force, functioning from heaven and manifesting itself in the universe.

Our genetic makeups and real identities lie under layers of human fleshy tissue. Our true nature is the spirit that is the heart of who we are. The body we live in is our earth suit, designed to survive in this world. The human flesh dies, but the spirit lives on through eternity. It's not impossible for our human spirit to live on this earth without a physical body. It's humanly impossible. Once a human is appointed to depart to the afterlife, the body must transform into spirit form. This is necessary before entering eternity since the human body is exposed to the corruption of sin. Our society was founded on God's morals, truths, and principles. As time progresses, those standards are becoming obsolete. It is morally wrong to omit God from our presence.

There are three facets to God: God omnipotent, God omniscient, and God omnipresent. Each one represents God's characteristics. God is self-subsistent, meaning he needs nothing outside himself. The highest infinite power of God is the omnipotent, the all-powerful one. God is the eternal source of energy, which sustains all things through the life flow of his unlimited power (New International Version [NIV]; copyright 1993, 1978, 19and 1984 by International Bible Society) or (Job 36:22-24 NIV).

The omniscient God perceives all things were created, and nothing is hidden without his knowledge, not even the intention of our hearts. The omnipresent God is present everywhere at the same time. No matter where you are in this life or the afterlife, he knows. Until our acknowledgment of God is embedded in our lives, we are spiritually destitute, forever searching for answers in the wrong places. Throughout the creation of humanity, human sins grieved God, and humankind became very rebellious (Genesis 6:6).

Since we are by-products of the first man—Adam— we are still affected by consequences of hatred, assassination, conflict, murder, and so on. The enemy is a multi-manipulator who lives up to his name while conning millions into playing his evil game. Without acknowledging the full revelation of who the devil really is, our world will self-destruct right before our eyes. If we can see the enemy's plans, we can change the course of life and the world around us. We are self-indulged in our abilities to understand that there are unseen evil forces among all humanity.

The enemy operates in the invisible spirit realm to obliterate souls belonging to God. We could debate whether Satan is real, but we can't negate the fact that the world is full of opposition. His name alone represents destruction for believers, and nothing good lies within him. The fact remains that he loves nothing more than causing division and misfortune in people's lives. Satan is the mastermind behind the evil in the world. If we are not careful, he can blind us into helping support his evil deeds.

The Bible depicts Satan as the invisible god of this world and prince of the power of the air (2 Corinthians 4:4; Ephesians 2:2 KJV). Therefore, he's within his legal right to control, operate, and skillfully manage this global system with the hope that the world's population will worship and praise his name. He has unlimited—though momentary— access over regions, nations, and territories.

It's ridiculous to assume you can engage the enemy on your own. It's more spiritual than you imagine. Humanity is no match against the unseen forces. It calls for God's intervention to unarm his opponents, working against the children representing the light. Ephesians 6:12 tells us the struggle is not against flesh and blood but against principalities and powers, against rulers and dominion, against spiritual wickedness in high places not of this world but in the heavenly realm. God is greater and more powerful than the devil. Jesus has proven this to be so by defeating him. If we refuse to heed to God's Word in our lives, we'll continually live a defeated life. We're in search of something much deeper, our hearts' desire to connect with something higher than ourselves.

The Lord tells us for whatsoever is born of God overcomes the world, and this is the victory that overcomes the world, even our faith. We are to overcome the world (1 John 5:4 KJV). To overcome the world is determined by your act of faith and the belief in God's word knowing that God will fight against what we can't see. This global system is the devil's social network and economic system, seeking jurisdiction over humanity on earth. It's illegal for the enemy to do anything without a willing soul to participate in his twisted demise. The enemy of our souls is continuously working against believers to steal their faith. The only way we're allowed to wrestle against the enemy is through speaking the Word of God and praying with all supplication, worship, praises, request, and fasting. Only then are you guaranteed overcoming victory.

CHRISTIAN ON THE FRONT LINE

My life was withering away right before my eyes. Turning into a stumbling block unable to see my way clearly. There were times I wondered if my life would've been different if I had stayed in Nevada. During these past years my eyes beheld the darkness that surrounded me. I was engaged in a spiritual warfare battle that was designed to distort the mind. I was exhausted and drained emotionally, physically, and mentally. Most of all, my faith was challenged, tempted, and tried. Depending on your specific spiritual battles it can become undeniably painful, perhaps the worst kinds of cruelty ever. I do not fight without my armor, which is the Word of God. Putting on the whole armor of God is like wearing a protective shield, a defense against the enemy. God's Word said, "Finally my brother be strong in the Lord and the strength of His might. Put on the full armor of God, so that you will be able to stand firm against the schemes of the devil" (Ephesians 6:10–11 KJV).

I now understand clearly that the enemy does nothing unless summoned by vile souls. If any branch of the military is not properly equipped for a war, chances are good it will lose the fight. The same is true for true born- again Christians. Therefore, all power belongs to Jesus; and Satan has limited power on Earth. Jesus gave believers that same power to defeat the enemy. It's important, as believers, to realize that same power is ours, and we need to walk in it every day. We are in a spiritual battle just to survive life. There are things in the atmosphere manifesting constantly which affect the way we live as well as other aspects of life. In all seriousness, being held captive by the evil one comes with a great responsibility because you must know and understand who you're dealing with. As true believers, Christ must be the focus point in our lives. There is no other way to win the war with the kingdom of darkness. You must be fully suited and arm yourself with God's word to be better equipped to war against the forces of evil.

It's a fact that morally wrong individuals hide behind the devil, and the devil hides behind wicked individuals. The enemy is masterful at camouflaging his falsehood making it appear as the truth. Too often, without reservation, we give the devil legal access to enter our lives. We do this through our carefree living standards and not knowing his deceptive devices. Collectively, humans take life for granted, neglecting the real purpose of life. Society has become separated from God, leaving him out of our lives. Most of us don't even revere God, Jesus, Holy Ghost, or his Word. However, they're unchangeable and can't be separated. God is omnipresent, and he sits high above the heavens while looking toward earth. This doesn't sound like he's absentminded. Nor is he incoherent about our affairs.

Most times, people go to great extremes to claim Christianity, with one exception. Some lack the two main ingredients—loving God and loving thy neighbor as thyself (Matthew 22:35–40). Woe unto those pretenders of righteousness, deceiving and mocking Christ's name. There will come a time when everything you thought you stood for, as well as your faith's foundation, will be challenged. Too many religious folks have the appearance of being godly, but their wayward thinking is worldly, childish, and arrogant.

The ungodly promote malice intention and thoughts within their hearts because they know not God. Genesis 6:5 explains, "God saw that the wickedness of man was great in the earth, and that every imagining of the thoughts of his heart was only evil continually." God gives treacherous men and women opportunities to redeem themselves from their iniquities. Christ desires that not a single soul perish, rather to seek to live unto eternity (John 3:16 KJV). Life is supposed to construct itself precisely as a means of rebuilding a firm foundation.

People can't seem to find common ground with each other. Could it be that we're too insensitive toward our peers who are having internal strife? Maybe we are too envious of others. Or could it be we're too busy finding faults and flaws instead of accommodating each other? If pretenders of righteousness, the ungodly, the wicked, or sinners knew they were being deceived by false impressions from the evil one, they would run as fast as they could to get away from him.

Living life solely for pleasure only leads to being deceived by the feeling of fleshly desire, ultimately leading to death. There is no discrepancy between being carnally minded and carnality. Both have a high aspiration to please the flesh. Being carnal is thinking in the ways of the world to entice immorality. Immorality is defined as the violation of moral laws, norms or standards. Immorality is normally applied to people or actions, or in a broader sense, it can be applied to groups or corporate bodies, beliefs, religions, and works of art. The Lord requires believers to work out their salvation with fear and trembling, including your old sinful nature and worldly intentions. Old habits are to be replaced with the mind of Christ Jesus.

Most born-again Christians are immature and carnally minded even after receiving salvation. Carnality is a state of mind having a strong desire to birth out what appeals to the flesh, even if it inappropriately comes because of one's actions. We live in a society where carnality has taken over the ability to restrain from our sinful natures or fleshly desires, but temptations keep us captive. Our bizarre behaviors stem from an unrealizable source unknown to humankind that manipulates the human concept of what is morally right and wrong. Satan encourages us to trust our own judgments and desires rather than trust God and his goodwill toward us.

The adversary appears to be a beacon of light to the world to capture the hearts of men. The enemy tempts us in many fashions especially when we least expect it. Temptation is defined as a desire to engage in short-term urges for enjoyment, which often leads to sin. He entices individuals by tempting them with material things that are pleasurable and appeal to the flesh. Beautiful things and people constantly surround us, so it makes temptation harder to resist for many. Christ has that thought in mind as well. He told believers to submit themselves to God, and resist the devil, and he will flee (James 4:7 KJV). To resist something or someone means to withstand, strive against, or refuse to accept. The word of God states, whosoever committed sin transgressed also the law: for sin is the transgression of the law (I John 3:4). Sin is an action; therefore sin is not activated until it's put into motion. God does not tempt us with sin. Many Christians want one foot in the sanctuary of God's glory and the other foot halfway toward secretly meeting demons. The enemy welcomes us openly and provides a life full of misery. Remember there is no greater or lesser sin; all sin is equal with God.

Many individuals who have leadership positions in our sanctuaries today are dishonest. Spiritually speaking, they are selfish! Our leaders lack spiritual quality and responsibility to discern spiritual matters. The Bible states that these individuals are either spiritually dead or spiritually immune concerning God's kingdom and his people. If Christian leaders are not discerning and prayerful enough to detect when a deceiver enters the sanctuary, the enemy will fellowship with the rest of us. And many believers can't recognize a demon spirit in operation. Leaders who are called by God are held accountable for their congregation.

Not all leaders are corrupt. I'm speaking to those who make up the fivefold ministry, such as apostles, prophets, pastors, teachers, evangelists, deacons, and ministers. Let's not forget the congregation. We can't possibly lead someone to Christ if our own morals aren't in right standing with God. The enemy of our souls is always working so why is the church on break? However, my experiences have given me the ability to detect such enmity.

Most believers will find out they lack the spiritual ingredients to maintain holy and righteous lives before God. Many believers are counterfeit Christians, living under false pretenses, false worshippers, and have false faith. They live under the delusion that God is false and absentminded. The major reason most people can't identify Satan as the culprit is because he is the dark entity, operating from spiritual perspectives. Let's make no mistake about this: Satan knew God was sending his only begotten Son to save humanity.

If God didn't send his Son, all of humanity was going to self-destruct. Jesus Christ coming was foretold in the Old Testament. Jesus came to remove power from the evil one and to expose the works of darkness. It's prevalent throughout the Old Testament that Satan tried hard to obstruct the birth of the Messiah. The devil is God's opposing force, so by being born, God's Son has already defeated the devil.

Lord, please let the eyes of true believers' understanding be enlightened that they might know what the hope of their true calling is, what the riches are of the glory of your inheritance in the saints, and the exceeding greatness of your power toward those who believe (Ephesians 1:18–19 KJV). God gives us free range to implement moral and ethical decisions instead of choosing to be juvenile in our decisions. Humans can't afford to continue making inappropriate decisions based on emotions rather than using a more ethical manner.

Everything in life is based on spirituality and the principles of God's laws, yet we abuse them. In truth, the world was spoken into existence by the Spirit of God. If you think about it, we are talking spirits living in physical bodies that house our spirits. For us to live in the physical world, God designed a special "earth suit" for humanity to survive and live. Without this, life in the physical world would be impossible.

God allows us to grow and develop spiritually through his Word by acquiring a deeper understanding of sound doctrine. During Christ's ministry on the earth, he taught his disciples spiritual principles as a way of life. God is trying to elevate his people to another dimension to be effective in spiritual warfare. The kingdom of darkness works so effortlessly to build strongholds and fortresses in people's minds. Our responsibility as God agents is to use our spiritual weapon, which is the sword of the Word, to interrupt Satan's ability to hold individual minds captive and to liberate them from such.

Many of us do not even realize we're up against unseen demonic forces every day of our lives. We think we know Satan, but in reality, we are plain ignorant for he is the god of this world. The world is always full of surprises; the devil is also full of surprises. But they are the same schemes, plots, and tricks he's used since the beginning of time.

Individuals in my neighborhood community had schemes, plots, and tricks, and they were blinded by the curiosity to get away with assassination. It's unlawful for the devil to operate in the earth realm without a human agent. Satan works his evil and trickery through people. People who oppose God and his work are Satan's sons and daughters. He loves nothing more than to cause division and mayhem in people's lives.

There are people right now who desperately need to be freed from the devil's stronghold, which holds them bound by circumstance. The testing and trials we endure can be lengthy but we can overcome them through faith. Our trials and tribulations in life are only temporary and do not define who we are as believers. Your faith determines this. Our trials and tribulations are only a testing of faith whether serious to non-serious; our faith carries us greatly through the process. We need every faithful follower of Christ to join forces to break down the barrier created by the evil one. The believer's objective is to advance the kingdom of God, take back our territory from the enemy, and bring souls into the kingdom. God is not obligated to manifest anything in your life except through his written Word.

If you are a true believer, chances are you will face calamity more often than an average saint. Trying circumstances rob us of our happiness. Even more, it may set us back. Learning from these experiences is the key to redirecting our lives, so they'll not be repeated. None of us are without fault, but our shortcomings shouldn't define us. For the sake of Christ, it's time to revere and seek him before it is too late. Once believers and nonbelievers attain knowledge and understanding in the Word of God, it's beautiful.

There are spiritual preparations to arming yourself with the armor of God: belt of truth, breastplate of righteousness, feet shod with the preparation of the gospel of peace, shield of faith, helmet of salvation, sword of the spirit, and prayer and supplication in the Spirit (Ephesians 6:10–18). The spiritual armor of God is protective gear against the enemy. The spiritual weapons can tear down any forces of evil sent against the body of Christ. Our human spirit needs to be reeducated and retrained to understand spiritual warfare. The living Word of God is more powerful, sharper, and mightier than any two-edged sword, piercing even to the division of soul and spirit, and of joints and marrow. It is a discerner of the thoughts and intents of the heart (Hebrews 4:12 NKJV).

Every day we're engaged in a spiritual battle, fighting for our survival, as well as for family, loved ones, possessions, and more. Once we recognize these unseen evil forces are operating in the land, we can possibly see the bottom line behind human motivation. Wrestling with the hidden is no easy task. It causes God to intervene in the war pitting Spirit against spirit. Satan aims to dethrone God's kingdom and Lordship. We know this is impossible and will never happen.

Our beliefs must be connected to the all-knowing, divine Creator God. God-armed forces are designed to battle with those of darkness. Only God and his warring angels can drive back the forces of darkness on our behalf. There is no time to be passive; we must be aggressive during warfare. This path of life is a spiritual war zone, a world full of darkness and despair. As believers, we're endowed with the same Holy Ghost power that Jesus had. Jesus gave us permission to use Holy Ghost power to do spiritual warfare against the enemy. The forces of God's armies hold back the forces of darkness, keeping them from destroying lives. There's not a day that goes by that you will find me without God's armor.

Our biggest opponent is the devil! Again, the devil influences people to do his bidding. They carry out these orders whether they are fully aware of it or not. Spiritual wickedness blends in with society, masquerading as darkness as though nothing is out of the ordinary. Therefore, the real enemy is not the people, although they are accountable for their endeavors. It's important to recognize the magnitude of the enemy. It's like filing a lawsuit against God's people. Individuals who are confronted with malicious intent have plenty of opportunities to receive help in battling against such cruelty.

Our defining moments occur as we face the real atrocities of life. This happens when everything negative starts to resurface from your past. Eventually, those unpleasant scenes begin to unveil past failures. Instantaneously and unexpectedly, sins intervene to keep one hell bound. It's better to deal with past sins. The adversary is the epitome of sin and the accuser of the brethren. Therefore he enters your mind with the present, past and the secret of your sins, that you think no one else knows except you. A moment of quiet, silent announcement within yourself, reviewing every sin committed, every disappointment, and even wrong you do to another. Listen, you can't undo the past, but you can learn to forgive yourself and move forward. The Lord can only undo what you confess in his presence with a sincere heart of repentance, meaning you change ungodly behaviors. Due to our ignorance, God forgives everything except blaspheming the Holy Ghost (Mark 3:29; Matthew 12:31 KJV). Blaspheming the Spirit of God is like saying he doesn't exist.

Life challenges always compel you to reexamine yourself, life, family values, and friends to deal with unresolved issues suppressed in the back of your mind. Your first reaction is to reminisce over every wrongful misdeed you ever committed. But mulling over your past is irrelevant to God. Having a repentant heart and changing your unethical lifestyle and ungodly behaviors are what matters to God. Value life, and take nothing for granted.

LIVING ARRANGEMENT

Relocating from Nevada to Georgia was a big transition of having to adjust from one state to another. The environment didn't give me any indication that something was disturbing. My mom and grandmother lived there for years. I was more than happy to relocate to be near my grandmother and finally assist her. I enjoyed my obligation as a wife, mother, and grandmother.

Moving into my community, everyone appeared to be cordial, well mannered, friendly, and even more than eager to lend a helping hand if necessary. What a deception! I wasn't too familiar with many locations or residences in my surrounding area. Living in a small community environment is rather different from life in the big city. After living here for more than sixteen years, I never suspected the unthinkable could occur in my seemingly nice neighborhood. I never thought anyone was vindictive enough to destroy another human being. I couldn't imagine individuals in my environment had so little regard for human life, especially mine.

I presented myself in a respectful manner when I met others through school, my job, place of worship, and even while shopping. Many of these people have ambushed and stabbed me in the heart spiritually. To think I befriended some of these fraudulent individuals, never considering my life was in jeopardy because of heartless souls.

You're probably wondering what I could have possibly done to deserve such calamity. Is there anyone the devil does like? Individuals who humiliated me were friends to my children or related to my grandchildren, nieces, or nephews. Some were even next of kin to my family. It's fascinating to think someone would maliciously hurt another for no apparent reason other than for selfishness. I'm learning people who deal with the occult have the ability to influence overly weak-minded individuals and make them do anything.

It's amazing how unidentified acts of evil disrupt life, hindering the probability of achieving happiness. I wouldn't give the enemies any satisfaction or give into their destructive plague. God's Word must be the basis of what we stand for and believe. Deuteronomy 31:8 states, "It is the LORD who goes before me. He will be with me; he will not leave me or forsake me. Do not fear or be dismayed."

The very ones you think will support you may end up disappointing you. There was no one trustworthy in my life other than a few family members, my pastor, and my spiritual mother. There was also a lack of trust since these vicious individuals undermined me and employed many souls to observe and pursue my every move. These perpetrators have influenced other individuals on their jobs to go even further; some of them truck drivers.

If I traveled out of town and state, the enemy was there. If I visited my children and other people's homes, the enemy was peeping and waiting for me to leave. If I wanted to pamper myself, the enemy was waiting, sitting right there. If I attended my house of worship, the enemy was also there. If I attended intercessory prayer, chances were the enemy would be sitting in the midst. If I prayed outside, the watchers thought I was completely insane. If I was outside communicating with family and friends, the perpetrators hurt me. If I left my home for any reason, the enemy did as well. Witchcraft is a vicious cycle monitoring your every move through networking of evil people traveling from town to town and state to state.

There was some crucial reasoning as to why I felt trapped in my environment. These people were adults, seniors, young and old, men and women. I trusted no one. I had never seen so many individuals, especially Christians, who were willing to believe lies rather than discern the truth. Beloved, never avenge yourselves, but leave it to the wrath of God, for it is written, vengeance is mine, I will repay, says the Lord (Romans 12:19 KJV).

HEARTBREAKING NEWS

I was entering extraordinary proof of the unexpected. I had to brace myself intensely for what lay ahead. It was a typical day when unexpected, heartbreaking news overtook us by storm, altering the pattern of our lives forever.

My daughter had four-year-old twin boys. Suddenly, the oldest succumbed to an unexpected death, leaving the family baffled about what happened. It was especially heartbreaking because I video chatted with them the previous night. The next day, he was gone, leaving us in despair. Everyone was traumatized by the loss of my grandson. A child departing this life early is not easy to cope with.

To me, it felt as though my life was gradually slowing down. I was working faithfully for the Head Start program as a substitute teacher. My core passion is to dedicate myself to helping children develop and succeed academically. My attitudes toward children never change because they help me keep smiling.

Even after the passing of my grandson, I never lacked responsibility working as a substitute teacher. I experienced multiple car accidents; two of those accidents happened before and after his death. I was under a physician's care for months. My pain was unbearable most days. I wasn't employed long enough to take leave, so I chose to keep working rather than quit. In most cases, working with tremendous aches and pain just added more problems. The only thing I could do was go to work, attend physical therapy, come home, and go to bed. My ability to maintain my home life was becoming completely overwhelming and tiresome at times. With much physical therapy, things finally returned to normal.

In the summer of July 2013, I was preparing to attend my niece's wedding. Summer break from school was ending, and I was still grief-stricken over the loss of my grandson. I had another automobile accident, and it almost cost my life. The driver was preoccupied, not paying any attention to the road, at thirty-five miles per hour. He hit my vehicle, totaling it. I was transported to a nearby hospital, traumatized and confused. I wondered if my granddaughter, who lived with me, were okay. I was devastated, so devastated I couldn't bear to live. I couldn't bear the thought of undergoing treatment again. Deeply disappointed over recurring injuries, depression was written all over my face. I received treatment under the care of a physician who treated me after my second automobile accident. Apparently, doctors couldn't understand why I wasn't getting any better; none of their treatments were working.

During my highs and lows, I desired to see my late grandson, except it was under false pretenses. This is what the Bible calls familiar spirit. The enemy loves to take advantage of our vulnerabilities and deceive us in our weakest and lowest moments. The adversary has the means to put into motion accidents, sicknesses, deaths, and other disturbances.

On four occasions, rebuking the demon spirits didn't always make them leave as expected. They would pretend to leave, giving false hope, only to find out some spirits lingered around even after being cast out. Most of the time, demon spirits are stubborn and refuse to release the person entirely. Therefore, rebuking these evil spirits is pointless. I do believe in the power of deliverance.

DECEIVED BY DECEPTION

I believe these three episodes had to happen in sequence to bind me to the spirit entity. The witch practitioners and her associates waited for the perfect opportunity to set up their deadliest ambush. If hell is like anything I've experience then it's not for me. Leading up to these events signs were present indicating something wasn't right but I paid them no attention. To me this was a normal part of my life. I realize my responsibilities and obligations were becoming overbearing but I've always manage to take care of business. Months after the burial of my grandson, I had three encounters with an unrevealed source manifest in my bedroom. Mysterious as this may sound, two of those phenomena occurred during the same week. Another incident followed the week after. Even though I had these episodes, it didn't seem as though I was being deceived by demon spirits. My days were normal; nothing was out of the ordinary, and no strange occurrences took place.

The first occurrence happened in October 2013, around 2 o'clock in the morning. I was unexpectedly awakened by some rather surprising slight movements. They were followed by what appeared to be a combination of footsteps, attempting to get comfortably into bed. Despite the fact the TV was on, the room was completely dark. It seemed like everything was motionless, and there was no communication whatsoever.

I was nervous, unable to move. I tried to figure out whether this experience was real. I was perplexed because I'd never experienced anything like this. Though I was nervous and tense, I was also rather calm. No one was in the room but me. Or so I thought. Lying quietly, I could barely move. I wondered, is my imagination playing tricks on me? After all, my late grandson would climb in bed next to me. I staggered to the bathroom, turned on the light, returned to bed, and everything was back to normal. There was no more paranormal activity, no movement or imprint, no more tiptoeing, and nothing disturbing. Turning on the light ceased all activity. Wasn't that unbelievable! I slept without any problem.

The thought never entered my mind that this was something evil. Realizing this paranormal activity was not normal, I tried to make sense as to why this was happening to me. I did think, this is something my grandson would do. I shared this experience with my husband and then the second experience with my youngest daughter.

The second occurrence happened on a typical day. I was running errands, cleaning, listening to music and lectures on my computer, and reading throughout the day and into the night. I was restless and unable to sleep, so I went back to the computer to listen to the teaching. Everyone had gone to bed except me; I often stayed up late, especially once everything had settled down. In my bedroom, my computer desk is less than halfway from the bathroom. Sitting next to my computer, I never left my chair other than to go to the bathroom. As I looked toward the bathroom door, I was dumbfounded by a rather unusual sight forming in my presence. Immediately, my heart started palpitating so rapidly, it sounded like a loud drum playing in my ears.

I was mesmerized by this vapor of grayish-white clouds manifesting before my eyes as if someone were smoking cigarettes. Out of this strange haze of clouds, the vapor began forming a picture frame. I felt like I was in a trance state, as though someone had hypnotized me so that I was unable to move. Once the frame was completely formed, a face appeared directly in its center. I recognized it as the face of my deceased grandson, I had no doubt. My grandson's appearance was so vivid, it wasn't hard to recognize him. He was beautiful and appeared to be happy. I could see him from head to waist, and the image was very detailed and felt real.

If I could describe the way he looked, it would be as we knew him before he left. I was unaware the devil was attempting to ensnare me by impersonating my grandson. I was extremely emotional and happy seeing his face. His facial features hadn't changed, but there was no actual color except for a grayish-white. As a matter of fact, the demon spirit was the spitting image of my grandson wearing a striped shirt. His gorgeous smile and bright eyes that light up the room. The way the familiar spirit entered the frame was exactly like the picture on my dresser.

Though I was immobilized, my heart palpitated fast, as if I were running a marathon. I had a telepathic conversation with him, but his only response was to shake his head left and right and up and down. Just think, the entire time he was smiling. I was so honored to see him. I was vulnerable and receptive to seeing my grandson. Demons mislead many people by transforming their demeanors and appearing as angels of light. The only thing these three occurrences brought me was a world of misery.

I was at my lowest state, but the thought never occurred to me to rebuke this deceiver impersonating my grandson. Once my grandson entered my room in the form of a smoky white cloud, I couldn't contain myself. The entire time he was all smiles because he was acknowledging the fact that I gave him access to enter my life, not realizing I was making the biggest mistake of my life. The enemy had me in the palm of his evil scheme. Once we were done communicating, I told him to go back to God, and he left suddenly.

I never experienced anything of this magnitude. The way the enemy deceived me was through what is called a familiar spirit, meaning the devil can impersonate your deceased loved ones, location, objects, or things familiar to you. My familiar spirit was disguised as my deceased grandson; it looked and smiled exactly like him. I was still brokenhearted and distraught over the loss of my grandson. I desired to see him, and nothing else mattered. The world of darkness seemed to be aimlessly perched over my head, attempting to smother the life force out of me. I was blinded by my emotional disturbance and clueless as to why I had these sudden urges to see my grandson. But despite everything that was happening, I was still content and continued to go about my daily routine. Don't ever believe the dead come back to earth. They don't. This is how the devil deceives many into thinking they can communicate with their deceased love ones. Take it from me, this is an attempt by the evil one to gain access into your life as well as that of anyone who is related to you.

Another incident occurred the following week. The third occurrence happened again in my room while I was lying down. When I woke up that morning, I was on my side, and it felt as though someone was behind me. My husband was across from me. Lying there, I thought, Not again! This is insane and too weird. I kept wondering whether my imagination was playing tricks on me. I held my breath, and to my surprise, something other than my husband was alongside me, moving. I couldn't see what it was, but it was real.

I didn't say anything to my husband right away because I thought, he's going to think I am crazy. Once I took the initiative to do some research on the wicked spirit, I opened up to my spouse. I silently wondered what the meaning of these experiences was; I didn't realize it was leading to something horrendous. Since things were becoming more bazaar and strange occurrences were surfacing, I took the initiative to attend church despite my circumstances.

One Sunday, I attended church as if nothing was unusual. I walked directly toward the altar. I knelt and prayed, crying out to God. My heart was so heavy. The praises were so intense because everyone was on one accord, seeking God for answers and solutions to their problems. Other saints were praying with such conviction and passion, having sincere hearts toward God's throne. God was my witness. While kneeling before the altar in prayer, the spirit entities jumped out of me. I felt light, whole, and free.

There was one disadvantage to returning home. Unfortunately, the problem was in my home, especially my room. My difficulties returned as soon as I entered my room. It was like those vengeful spirits never left. It was where the enemy deceived me three times. No one knew except for my husband. When I returned home, these same spirits returned. I was too humiliated; I felt as though I did this misdeed to myself.

It was quite difficult to sleep under these conditions, especially during the night hours, without some commotional uproar. There were many days my sleeping pattern was disturbed by unwanted evil spirits. Sleeping was obsolete due to waking up most mornings feeling completely strange and different. I felt weighed down, unable to free myself. My physical body felt overloaded by something dreadful. Changes also took place in my mind. I kept wondering what am I being controlled by?

I stayed awake mostly. It felt very unsafe and weird living

there. God, what is this, and who wants to hurt me? I prayed to the Lord to help me since my soul was perplexed, and I didn't know what was going on. I begged God, Do not let them tear my heart to pieces for their hearts are evil and wicked day and night. One thing I know how to do is call on God for help. He is the only one who can deliver me.

PHYSICAL EFFECT

Following the last occurrence in October, everything started to change for the worst. I was starting to feel indifferent about myself. My body began to have physical changes. There was never a dull moment. I never knew what to expect. I didn't understand why things were happening. I was clueless.

I felt as though something diabolical was transpiring within me. Unexplained things were taking place, and it was as though I was watching a scary movie unfold. I was frightened. If you faced wickedness in your darkest days, perhaps you would be frightened too. Negative, vengeful spirits invaded my presence. Normally, this is unreal. Who on earth is capable of such cruelty as this?

I learned witchcraft was sent in the form of black magic and several other kinds of magic to interrupt all aspects of life. Male and female witches and associates sending demon spirits, I guess this was their way to assure that their twisted plan wouldn't fail. I know people are capable of all sorts of evil, but I asked, "Why now?" I didn't know what to think of this; I guess you could say I was in shock.

I experienced the worst forms of torture, agony, and grief

imaginable. Unable to sleep most days, spirit entities attached themselves to my flesh, my bedroom, property, and my home without my permission.

I didn't quite understand why it was happening. As mysterious as this may sound, demon spirits have supernatural powers, and they tried their best to control my thoughts and behaviors in every way possible. But I kept telling Satan, "The blood of Jesus is against you," or, "I am covered under the blood of Jesus." If you fight the unseen using your natural ability, you will be defeated every time. I had gone through significant changes over the previous years after enduring such madness.

This was nonsense. A whole army of enemies was against me, but getting rid of my presence wasn't going to be easy. God's enemies had evaluated me and deemed me as biodegradable, thinking I was a simple target to eliminate. They underestimated the power of the living God who dwells in me. There wasn't anything attractive regarding these unsettling frightening events.

Hardly any neighbors lived on my street in my deceitful community neighborhood, except for my mom and maybe a few others. Before the paranormal dramas unfolded, it was crucial for the evildoers to remove any unknown, possibly unreliable source from the property. My mom was leasing the property to a close relative. Disagreements sporadically erupted, causing some division. Eventually, the tenant moved out, leaving no known witnesses to their crime of obsession.

My grandma had been deceased for years. Hardly anyone visited her while she was alive except for her children, grandchildren, and great-grandchildren. On occasion, her ex-husband or sister-in-law visited. Two young boys pretended to visit my grandma knowing she had been deceased for years. These terrible people in my neighborhood were making sure no one else was left on the scene. These ungodly souls managed to come up with all sorts of approaches to make sure there were no witnesses who could identify them. It makes plenty of sense to remove people who possibly could recognize them and replace them with heartless and ruthless individuals just like them. Since we have no neighborhood watch, what better way to have plenty of access to roam the vicinity of my yard without any interruption and do what pleases them. The frightening thing was they even silenced my two dogs, eventually killing one.

This whole witchery scheme was messy and planned. What the enemies weren't expecting was that my fight and determination to survive was very strong. I noticed some rather unusual events unfolding before my eyes. Perhaps it was a coincidence, or was my imagination deceiving me? I prayed and prayed, asking God, "Why is this happening to me?" Practically every evil device planted around my home was a trap for my downfall.

These ungodly individuals would stare as though the ultimate crime was committed. They hated Jesus Christ for no real reason other than they were influenced by the evil one. Some of these perpetrators and their comrades appeared more than eager to speak and be friendly toward me. To do evil toward another and then pretend to be friendly, like nothing is happening, gives me the impression of just how demonic and imprudent one is.

OUTRAGEOUS NEIGHBORS

Apparently these astonishing acts of injustice were essentially staged to achieve willful desire as a conspiracy portrayed by agents of the rebellious. Living like normal, my husband and I were raising our grandchildren. Honestly, I was frightened because strange phenomena were taking effect after my personal encounters with the invisible.

I remember the day this nightmare started to unfold. I received a rather unusual phone call condemning me for something that had happened thirty-four years ago.

Nervously sitting on the steps, having a conversation with my baby brother, scores of outrageous neighbors filled with malice intent flooded the street. I sensed something dreadful was about to go down.

Onlookers drove their automobiles, some randomly walked by, and others casually rode their bikes past our house. Unless you lived here, you would think the neighborhood was having a marathon. Though I did not understand why all the disturbances were surrounding me, I sensed it had something to do with me. It felt like death was in the atmosphere. It was an awkward, eerie feeling. I wasn't feeling like myself; it was the feeling something unknown was operating against me.

These individuals stayed on my street for quite some time. I could feel animosity surging in the atmosphere. Darkness seemed to appear from every direction, eager for me to recognize its presence.

The thought of witchcraft working against me never entered my mind. I was on edge mentally and physically, my body was undergoing some significant changes, and uncertainties were happening all around me. My brain was wearing thin; confusion plagued my common sense and judgment. There was no time to waste. The devil was trying to make sure I would never fulfill my ambitions, goals, and dreams. Trust me; it's very frustrating to know that something like an evil spirit can cause so much suffering. Important facts to remember evil spirits do not enter the body physically; they only attach themselves to a body spiritually. They are disembodied spirits that desire to inhabit a person body by attaching themselves. Their aim is to oppress or either, ultimately taking a complete control over the persons will by possessing the body. It's illegal for a demon spirits to operate on the earth realm without a person to attach it to.

I was too ashamed to talk to anyone about what I felt was going on. Besides, they wouldn't comprehend my situation. When trying to explain your complicated situations to someone, the grimness on his or her face says everything. Unfortunately, many people think you are mentally deranged because such talk is unheard of; people aren't used to hearing such talk. The entire purpose of doing evil against someone is to cause the person's demise by any means necessary.

I was suffering in silence, wondering who was going to rescue me. No one notices such cruelness except the perpetrators. I was clueless as to why these sudden changes had occurred in my physical body. But as I said earlier, not only was my body changing, but I had inappropriate thoughts and desires. I felt like the biggest failure. My self-esteem was reduced to nothing.

The only thing I knew to do was attend my home church. I admit being so eager to be in the presence of God that I couldn't arrive at church quickly enough. Though praises and worship were already in place, I headed straight to the altar. Without any hesitation, I cried out to God to help me. I didn't tell anyone, not even my pastor, what was wrong. I felt it was my fault. The feeling in the church was powerful.

When I awoke Monday morning, all hell was breaking loose. I felt intensely weird sensations, as if something strange was taking over my mind and body. The force of an invisible entity controlled and manifested itself through me spiritually. I frantically paced in a state of desperation, trying everything imaginable to protect myself.

I took the initiative to call my aunt and explained what was happening. She prayed with me and gave me words of encouragement. After communicating with my auntie, a sense of peace came over me, but only momentarily. I was sitting in a recliner, having a conversation with my husband, when I suddenly felt the unrevealed entity lift me off the chair. Even amid experiencing the paranormal, I politely asked my husband to throw me something heavy to keep me from lifting off the chair. So we now knew spirits were extremely strong.

The feelings of entrapment and helplessness were becoming too overwhelming for me to handle alone. Yes, my husband was aware of these strange transformations.

This was a nightmare come to torment my very presence. This manifestation of demon spirits wasn't my forte. And my husband couldn't completely understand. So I suffered in silence. No one could hear my heartfelt cry. I wondered, When will my end come? And I prayed.

It doesn't matter what anyone may say, these encounters were scary as hell (excuse my French). Prior to these most shocking events, I had seen and experienced ghosts, demonic spirits, and animalistic spirits throughout my home. Various articles on the Web state demonic forces are sent by witches, sorcerers, and wizards. They try to fight you and enter your body.

Our future is forever confronted by uncertainties of our world, wreaking havoc in the land. Some humans have become coldhearted and heartless toward other people. These individuals are within our communities, churches, workforces, business establishments, and playgrounds. And some live right next door. Worst of all, we worship together. Yes, there are evildoers in the sanctuary, possibly wishing you evil. Apostles, pastors, priests, prophets and prophetess, evangelists, ministers, deacons, and members of the congregation are sent to our churches to undermine God's people and cause problems.

HOME INVASION BY EVIL SPIRITS

Nothing ever happens in this earthly realm without human involvement, including evoking the underworld to facilitate their evil conspiracies. Looking back over my life, I now understand how certain incidents worked against me. The enemy's motive was to expel my existence from birth until present, and it all now makes sense. Transitioning from one state to the next came at a high price. Previously undisclosed secrets were exposed by harsh reality camouflaged under false appearances.

My disposition came without warning as a whirlwind, moving in for the kill, suddenly altered the plans and course of my life and family. I used to wonder why God allowed me to survive and live. I was plagued with the dark side, which came to hound my existence.

As my life was unraveling, I was inspired to write a daily journal, capturing every moment and detail of real-life changing events. Being demoralized by demonic forces mentally, physically, and emotionally came as a death threat.

Imagine living life respectfully and smoothly and then suddenly, darkness lies at your residence.

Listen, no black magic of any kind is proficient at outpowering the almighty God. My home was the main attraction for the supernatural. It was plagued by malevolent spirits. Angry spirits, revengeful spirits, sewage spirits, seducing spirits, and spirits of discord all took up residence in my home. The atmosphere would be peaceful and then gradually disappear into the darkness, bringing back chaos. Unseen spirits entities traveled outside their district and landed on my property. I had no explanation as to why this was happening or what I did to cause this intentionally cruel and vengeful retaliation.

As unfamiliar things surfaced, my eyes experienced their fair share of supernatural demons. These disfiguring objects resonated inside and outside the home. I saw unexplainable images and objects on walls, couches, the ceiling, and in midair. Objects appeared and then disappeared, sounds came from nowhere, and sleep was not on my side. Demon spirits are dark black, and their eyes are red, like those of an alien. And they're incredibly daunting. That would be enough to cause anyone to lose it.

Once, while sleeping in my husband's room, I awoke to the sight of a tall bronze statue. The light was out in his room, and the only light was coming from the hallway. While I sat there, this illusion of a tall Iron man standing looking in the opposite direction of me appeared.

Seeing orbs was another common sign of the perpetrators,

alerting me of their presence. Orbs are energy forms. They are bright white color and round. It didn't matter what I was doing; orbs zoomed across my eyes.

These dark souls were disgusting and had no respect. My dogs were sensitive to seeing spirits and constantly barked and turned in circles for no obvious reason. There were all sorts of evil devices planted around the property, the corner street of my home, and more, I'm sure. There were nails, glass, coins, chip particles, wood, manure, rocks, tons of dirt, leaves, white or blue scratch paper, strange smells, bugs, and more. Now I recognize these objects were placed there to help the evil spirits to fulfill their obligation of causing harm.

The presence of evil was everywhere, like scenes, from a horror film. I felt trapped and helpless in circumstances that were becoming too big for me to handle alone especially during the night. I had never seen spirits in my life until now. Seeing ghostly images is out of the ordinary, and this, too, overwhelmed me.

This manifestation of evil spirits and demons was a nightmare come to torment my very presence. To others, you're delusional, but the whole purpose of doing evil against someone is to cause his or her demise. In the early stages of my tribulation, it was pointless to close my eyes. Rather than observing nothing but pure darkness, I witnessed horrible images of ugly faces.

It was difficult to sleep during the night without some commotion. So I remained mostly awake. Living here felt very weird. "God, what is this, and who wants to hurt me?" I prayed. I asked the Lord to help me because my soul was perplexed, not knowing what was going on. "God, do not let them tear my heart to pieces, for their souls are evil and wicked day and night." One thing I know how to do is call on God for help.

When I awoke most mornings, there would be something different and strange about me, causing me confusion. The spirits had a grip on me and tried their best to keep me under their control, unwilling to release me. I couldn't eat anything. All I could think about was that I felt differently. My room would be cold as ice; it was so cold I couldn't stand to be there. I wrote my husband a note, telling him, "I am scared, frightened, nervous, and trembling. Spirit demons are attempting to control my mind." I was hostile. Nothing fazed me except the death of my grandson. I kept telling my husband, "I can't live like this. What's the use?" These evil spirits were in full operation, leading me to self-destruction. The aroma of death plagued the atmosphere and peace was nowhere to be found. The worst things were feeling indifferent and losing my ability to comprehend what was going on.

Losing my grandmother was mind-blowing, but the notion of ending my life never was in question. I never had a visitation from my deceased grandma.

Through the work of male and female witchcraft practitioners and their associates, I was headed for doomsday. Every entrapment was an attempt to keep me bound under demonic control. I wrote a short synopsis of my experiences and information attained through this process. Everything evil started to unfold and the rest of the story came into play against my will. I had no idea why this immorality was happening. I found it odd that these occurrences happened after my grandson's passing. Now my only option was to seek prayers and be in God's presence.

Animals were used as sacrifices. Ceremonial rituals and parties were thrown to invoke the demon spirits. Evil presences surrounded me no matter where I happened to be. I was prone to seeing the faces of evil spirits and sensing evil presences around people. They loved to frighten me during the night, and that they loved to do their dirty deeds at midnight sounds a lot like criminal activity. I've heard demons communicate in their own languages in phone conversations with other people. The scariest things are dark spirits. They are wicked, evil, horrible, disgusting, and frightening to the point of driving a person insane.

Every evil device planted around my home was to lead me to my downfall. These were supposed to be productive citizens in my local environment and surrounding area. But these ungodly souls stared at me, amazed that I wasn't disfigured.

There is a pecan tree not too far from my window. Throughout my calamity, a couple of colorful snakes were planted in the tree stump outside, next to my bedroom window, in hope of biting me. I routinely walked around the property praying, and accidentally came across the snakes. Light always overshadows darkness, so my praying was a snare to them. The danger of this was that my grandchildren were subject to the hidden traps outside.

There were plenty of moments when my imagination deceived me into thinking something was real when, in fact, it wasn't. Witchcraft deceives the mind through planting false perceptions.

Some ignorant perpetrator routinely silenced my dogs, so we were unaware of any crime taking place outside. Sometimes I thought it was my imagination, playing with my mind. But the episode with the colorful snakes in my yard and hidden in the tree was not the first time. The snake looked too real to be fake. I am also aware something is buried in my yard. Plenty of booby traps were set up in my honor, but the Holy Spirit always made me aware of these hidden dangers.

I live in a pecan grove, and I used to take pride in knowing my trees would blossom during springtime. But over time, the leaves were slowly destroyed by negative energies surging through the atmosphere. Negative spirits had the appearances of many unusual faces in the trees. It was obvious those unattractive spirits were camouflaging their identities among the trees' leaves and branches. When night arrived, the ground was always outlined with images of ghostly figures. There was always something strange and different about the trees. It felt like they had a message. I never paid trees any attention until now. If you ever notice trees take on the appearances of faces either naturally or by someone carving. Each tree has an untold story to communicate.

Unclean occult birds were assigned to surround the property, watching my every move. It was as if they were spying on me or signaling the witch or associates. No matter where I was, unclean birds always alerted others of my location. The sound of loud thumping and banging close to my bedroom window was a warning so that I was aware of their presence. Unclean birds as well as other animals would prowl around the house. Cats and dogs would stare uncontrollably as if they were human. Nevertheless, no occult dogs, cats, birds, chickens, cows, or horses were powerful enough to come against Jesus Christ's authority. Using the name of Jesus spoke volumes to the witches, warlocks, and animals.

Whenever foes placed objects in close range, I always had a reaction. Especially loud sounds—I mean extremely loud sounds directly penetrating my ears. The worst was loudness caused by drums, music, cars, trucks, and trains. These perpetrators knew from their spells, magic, and voodoo that loud sounds would trigger an extremely intense reaction in me. My heart would palpitate fast, causing me to be tense, nervous, have panic attacks, and become unbalanced. I was unable to cope. My head always ached; my physical body was in intense pain and underwent changes. I always had uncontrollable spells of emotional crying because I was miserable.

As soon as I discovered the objects in the yard and prayed over them the symptoms were immediately terminated. My symptoms stopped until the foes did something else stupid. Holy water, salt, speaking the Word of God, fasting, anointing oil, and ammonia were the cures for every unclean thing. It disinfected my home as well as made the evil spirits vanish. Because I used these items as a means of protection, especially outdoors, the evil ones thought I was doing the same wickedness as they. No, it was only to disintegrate evil entrapment. But the perpetrators were bold and unashamed.

Unlike their father, the devil, they hid their identities behind tinted windows. As I mentioned previously, there wasn't anything I could do without someone watching my every move. Basically, all these evil things happened right under our noses and mainly at night. At other times, they waited until no one was home. My mail was often tampered with, sometimes at the post office, United Postal Service, and other times at my residence. According to the law, this is a federal offense.

The craftiness of the community is that, out of absolute ignorance, most people band together, unaware that evil spirits distort and manipulate their minds. Unless they themselves are the witches. They did all sorts of things to assist unknown sources who offered them revenge on someone— money, or anything else the evil people desired. The Lord doesn't deal with evil; he deals only with the just and righteous. God is against the wicked. We willfully damage and destroy our own people without any justification. Instead of letting God handle the situation, we take matters into our own hands. The people you're creating the problem for is clueless to why this rudeness is happening.

LIFE-DEFINING MOMENT

Thanks to the Most High God for the battles he fought in the heavens on my behalf. God has spoken throughout my story. Thanks to those who endured with me throughout the end, God was speaking through my story. Thanks to those who thought less of me, God was speaking throughout my story. To those without understanding, God was speaking throughout my story. Thanks to those who rejected me without cause, God was speaking through my story. Thanks to those who persecuted and hated me without legitimate cause, God was talking to you through my story. I thank God for allowing me to weather through the storm of uncertainty.

My deepest expression of myself is to be precise and truthful to the best of my ability. Since my good characteristics are presently on the front line, I don't wish to fabricate lies. Nor do I desire to gain recognition. Rather, my goal is to expose the hidden dangers behind irreligious individuals employed as agents of rebelliousness. They could not destroy my soul. Satan and his rebellious children were limited to what God allowed. First Samuel 15:23 states, "For rebellion is as the sin of witchcraft, and stubbornness is as iniquity and idolatry. Because thou hast rejected the word of the Lord, he hath also rejected thee from being king." I rose above my circumstances in complete submission to the Holy Ghost's instructions, but not without a battle.

It gives me the liberty to thank everyone who had an active role—positive or negative—in bringing about my divine calling and purpose of God for my life. Defaming my person was a part of their perverted games to delude loved ones, friends, and even strangers into thinking I was insane. I witnessed many wicked deeds manifest right before my eyes, gripping my heart with pure disappointment.

Many questions arose. I was unaware of how to unravel the meaning of these heinous misdeeds. The real essence of my life story involves repulsive and terrifying events that momentarily and unexpectedly intervened. I realize the enemy blinds the minds of individuals who are easily persuaded. He uses them as pawns to participate in his twisted schemes. God does not create atrocities, but he will intervene in a person's life to bring about a greater good. It appeared my future was uncertain; no words could describe my deepest feelings. There I was, serving God faithfully. I am passionate toward righteousness and desired nothing to do with unrighteousness. There was no time to waste.

I was stripped completely down to nothing, and everything I valued was no longer important to me. I felt strange and uneasy. It was as though something was trying to restrain my ability to function most of the time. Demonic forces came as a death threat to demoralize me through physical abuse and manipulation. I wasn't alone. Innocent lives across the nation are being specifically targeted by the spirits of witchcraft. When someone desires to intentionally harm you through witchcraft spells etc., their main objective is to curse everything meaningful to you. The purpose of the enemy is to have you, destitute, insane, helpless, poverty stricken, isolated, sick, unemployed, with no one to confide in or speak into your life, to have disputes within marriages, to have unnecessary conflict between relationships, to have distance and alienation toward your relatives, to be without contact with others. They also cause people to be unruly for no reason. If they can Succeed in sabotaging your life by deliberately causing economic setbacks or any one of the above, everything seems hopeless even to the point of death. These are evil spirits in operations to sabotage a person's livelihood by killing, stealing and destroying. Remember Gods word is greater and more powerful than anything the devil and his demons can attempt to do and they are subject to the Lord Jesus Christ.

Because I encountered severe torture by male and female witchcraft practitioners and associates, it was a struggle to survive; this struggle became my norm. Imagine living life respectfully and smoothly, and suddenly darkness occupies your home. Threatening forces of wickedness led me to the invisible world of demons, evil spirits, apparitions, and ghosts of the worst breed. Lock me up; everything was overbearing and too intense.

I was confronted with spiritual darkness and plagued with

evil, venomous snakes in the most intensifying way, turning everything that meant something to me upside down. Despite the odds against me, I surprisingly exceeded my expectations of myself. My incentive to fight for my inherited right to survive was God's promise to me. My enemies were constantly thinking of ways to obliterate my existence. The enemy was my roadblock, but God was my sustainer and keeper.

I was unbelievably overshadowed beyond reason; my comprehension was invalid. Death, persecution, humiliation, evil eyes, slander, verbal curses, mistreatment, and suffering regularly stared me in the face. I felt isolated unto myself. My strength slowly drifted into thin air. I felt like a foreigner, wandering in an unknown wilderness, distant from family and friends.

The spirit of bewitchment disturbed our marriage, home, and grandchildren, causing conflict and separation within the home front. If my husband and I go our separate ways or move, the enemy has won. I refused to allow that to happen or give up! My marital relationship desperately needed to be reconciled, or we were both doomed. Without warning, tension and stress-related problems had moved in, causing us to have discord, hardship, difficulties, and to be insensitive toward each other. But through persistent prayers and staying before the Lord, we managed to overcome those difficult moments.

Throughout this entire process, the enemy attacked my total

body with the most intense pain possible. I was extremely exhausted, overburdened, overworked, and worn out from never-ending exhaustion. I endured severe mental and physical trauma. No human deserves such cruelty; animals receive more respect. It's amazing to now have maximum use and capacity of my mind and body without internal damage.

It's very clear Satan's chief objective is to weaken an individual's mind through control, replacing it with immoral behaviors. Apparently, my mind is no different; he deliberately attacked my mind, head, neck, and back with a severe burning sensation. I struggled to keep my sanity intact. The mind is truly a terrible thing to waste at the hand of someone other than yourself. To hold you captive, the enemy penetrates the mind by using a negative energy's substance to control and overshadow your mind. These negative attributes are used to cause suffering. I expand on that later.

Only God has the capability to liberate those who desire help from the onslaught of our tormentors. In many instances, sleeping became obsolete, strange, and unpleasant because entities appeared regularly in my room. I was in a place of confusion, randomly searching for clarity. I couldn't seem to shake the awkwardness of discontentment. The spirits had a grip on me, trying their best to keep me under their control. The worst was feeling indifferent and unable to think clearly.

Since fear was the primary factor here, the pressure of feeling as though something was happening always triggered heavy pressure in my chest, followed by nervousness, trembling vibrations, and anxiety deep in the pit of my stomach. In other words, it feels as though you've either taken the wrong medication or too much, causing you to be hyperactive.

Throughout my body, there were grinding sensations, as if a motor was running nonstop. It was annoying and painful. I heard unusual sounds coming from the depths of my stomach, as though some species embedded inside was searching for an open door. Those fears had me bound to the core, and once they were activated, I was constantly on edge and having insecurity issues.

Spiritual fear was deeply rooted and a constant trigger of panic. It was a fear that couldn't be seen or controlled by doing one simple thing. It was something I had to fight to get rid of. I was bound by circumstances and unable to free my mind from thinking something drastic was going to take place.

This type of fear is sent by someone doing spells to keep you on edge. In the natural world, spiritual fear is not caused by circumstances. It is caused by people with evil intentions. There's a big difference between fear embedded inside your physical body and fear of the unknown. It's like you're constantly bound, unable to move; as though something awful is going to happen. On the other hand, fear of the unknown is experiencing worry, anxiety, and problems, or having unpleasant feelings.

Remember—the enemy feeds off your fears, using them to terrorize you and gain control over your mind. My aim was to stay as positive as possible, but sometimes that became impossible. Over time, I managed to control such outbursts.

Isaiah 54:54 says that "No weapon that is formed against thee shall prosper; and every tongue that shall rise against thee in judgment thou shalt condemn. This is the heritage of the servants of the Lord, and their righteousness is of me, saith the Lord." I presented myself appropriately, without giving the impression of being uneasy. The spirit of fear had such a stronghold over me, and fear stared me in the face daily. I was uncomfortable being around people, even attending my church. Of course, I loved attending my Church, but it was becoming slightly unpleasant and uncomfortable because I knew individuals had malice in their hearts toward me. For various reasons, many souls attend church with malicious intentions, appearing blameless while their hearts are mischievous. Such individuals are undercover agents, secretly operating under demonic influence, enslaved to their iniquities.

It was very strenuous most Sundays, sitting in the service without drawing attention to myself. The pain was intense, sitting agitated and pretending nothing was happening while silently praying, asking God to protect me. I often cringed when I had to greet or hug someone in the sanctuary, not that I was antisocial. No matter how intense the pain, seeking medical attention was always pointless since this was spiritual, from the beginning.

Every day I endured suffering for my love and compassion for God. Such wickedness is not being exposed or detected in our churches. Either we are spiritually blindfolded or simply in denial. There were many opponents who employed other opposing individuals to follow in their twisted ways. My opponents didn't believe God's presence is always with me, resides within me, and lives through me, keeping me protected.

I figured out the reason these ungodly individuals kept driving by day and night. The evil spirit was attracted to sounds that caused a reaction within my physical body. I finally understood the reason behind the rapid palpations; I was under severe spiritual attacks. It didn't matter whether in my home, attending church, shopping, driving, traveling, or visiting. It was a never-ending story. Through research, I discovered the offenders were using a concentration called contagious magic and more. I'll explain later. Demon spirits are things you hear about in sermons, but rarely do you hear about how to deal with them.

There's power in the name of Jesus, so we must command the negative spirits to leave in his name. Christ has given the saints authority and powers to command the enemy to leave our presence. If someone doesn't know God or his existence, the individual is lost and defenseless. There's an enemy who's bigger than I, than you, could ever imagine. The eternal God and his host of Angels are the only ones who can battle and conquer spiritual forces, Satan, evil spirits and spiritual wickedness of this world, both on Earth and the spiritual realm. Fear thou not; for I am with thee: be not dismayed; for I am thy God: I will strengthen thee; yea, I will help thee; yea, I will uphold thee with the right hand of my righteousness (Isaiah 41:10 KJV).

DARK MAGIC AND DEMONIC SPIRITS

It is impossible to detect the devil in a visual sense. Rather, he can be detected through spiritual insight. It appears the enemy conceals his intention of immorality through atmosphere and people. Humanity aimlessly fights against each other rather than find the source or root cause. The Bible indicates we do not wrestle against flesh and blood but against the rulers, against the authorities, against the cosmic powers over this present darkness, against forces of evil in the heavenly places (Ephesians 6:12). It's noted that low-level demon spirits instigate nonhuman intelligence involving witchcraft and operate as agents of evil entities. They often disguise themselves so that we are under false impressions. Belial is known as the vilest and wickedest spirit in The Kingdom of Darkness.

I have gained some insight and knowledge concerning spells, magic, witchcraft, demonic spirits, evil spirits, ill-religious spirits, and more. Let's clear some misconceptions as to whether magic can affect people. Yes, I believe, being victimized myself, that magic does affect human nature to some degree. According to the Bible, demonic spirits are known as fallen angels who rebel against God (Revelation 12:4 KJV).

I would like to clear up the misconception that a true believer can't be possessed or demonically oppressed unless he or she refuses to fight. A true believer is not completely controlled by demonic spirits. However, if a believer refuses to wage war and stand up for his or her rights, the individual can become demonized by the evil spirit. Demonic forces (demon spirits) can attack the body causing illness, depression, financial difficulty, abnormal fear, etc. So, it is a good idea to be aware of the things that can open up a person to spiritual oppression.

On the other hand, nonbelievers are subject to demonic possession. It is true that demon spirits can enter the body through an open door through sin, trauma, séances, divination, drug paraphernalia, alcohol, occult involvement, Ouija broad, necromancy, witchcraft, and so on. According to an article I read, it states, "a complete demonic possession is a state in which one or several demonic spirits have gained access to an individual's body and then proceeds to take full control of the person's will. In such a condition, the demonic spirits use the person's body to express its personality and to carry out its evil intent. (http://www.demonic.name/demonic-possession).

Demonic oppression and demonic possession share some common interests. They both want to control a person's mental capacity and physical body by imposing afflictions and suffering, and more. Demonic oppression inflicts the body with unnecessary discomforting pain and suffering, but the person is in no way controlled by evil spirits. Demons can also use the force of influence to tempt individuals.

Demonic possessed is described as being under complete control of an evil spirit. The spirit usually takes control over the mind, body, and personality of the individual. The goal of the evil one is to control the mind and everything else relating to you. There are various reasons a person might become possessed. Sometimes it comes through rebelliousness, opening a door, having a reprobate mind, or a willingness to yield the soul as a down payment for material gain. And, of course, it can come through some form of spell work.

Wicked spirits are strongholds that tend to cause a person to have drug addiction, alcohol addiction, sex addiction, unforgiveness, hostility, sickness, diseases; the list goes on. God can set us free from any strongholds controlling our lives. A stronghold is a means to keep a person held captive by conditions. It's a power struggle of the mind, thoughts, and imagination. Evil spirits manipulate these strongholds to manifest in a person's life. The Bible indicates in 2 Corinthians 10:3–5, "For though we walk in the flesh, we are not waging war according to the flesh. For the weapons of our warfare are not of the flesh but have divine power to destroy strongholds. We destroy arguments and every lofty opinion raised against the knowledge of God, and take every thought captive to obey Christ." Witchcraft attacks the mind with imagination, confusion, sense of futility, suicidal thoughts, control, and so on.

An alternative form of magic used against an individual is black magic. It is used to cause harm to someone out of pure jealousy, vengeance, egoism, greed, and negativity. Harmful magic is detrimental to the mind and body as it tends to send an illusion, thereby deceiving someone. The enemy is crafty, and his aim is to sabotage your life by any means necessary. Bear in mind the enemy doesn't care for anyone. Even if a person doesn't necessarily believe in spell magic, it doesn't mean it won't take effect.

Christ is my life although evil was present through the working of spell magic that affected me against my will. Many of the adversary's weapons may form against you, but it doesn't have to overtake you. True believers can't be overtaken by enemy attacks unless they choose to give up the battle instead of being persistent despite opposition. Once a spell magic has been placed on someone, it's a curse.

Thanks to computers and our vast technology, the Internet is a magnet for obtaining information. Therefore, there is a lot of general information on magic, such as witchcraft magic, black magic, Santeria magic, white magic, candle magic, potion magic, contagious magic, sympathetic magic, and voodoo magic. There are a variety of articles, books, and magazines on the topic of magic. The Internet provides easy access to reading, learning, or purchasing. It doesn't matter what type of magic one desires; it's available.

Magic is used in many cultures for healing, keeping away evil, seeking the truth, and for vengeful purposes. Different cultures around the globe possess their own special methodology for performing specific rituals to invoke gods or goddesses for a precise objective.

Witchcraft is identified with the practice of having magical power and casting spells for various purposes. Specially made formulas create the desired results. Witchcraft is recognized as the art of using magical power to affect a person, place, or thing. The deed of practicing magic is well known for its ingredients and mixtures. But thanks to the use of computer technology, discovering the formulas is no longer a secret. The most dangerous form of black magic is the systematic perversion of occult power for the gratification of personal desire. Its less complex and more universal form is human selfishness for selfishness is the fundamental cause of all worldly evil.

A person will exchange his or her eternal soul for temporal power. Down through the ages, a mysterious process has evolved that enables one to make this exchange. In its various branches, the black art includes nearly all forms of ceremonial magic, necromancy, witchcraft, sorcery, vampirism, and many others. Also included under the same general heading are mesmerism and hypnotism, except when used solely for medical purposes, and even then, there is an element of risk for all concerned (the secret teaching of mysticism, paranormal, or sorcery). Undoubtedly, spirits of the underworld are summoned either by a magician or sorcerer performing acts of malevolence to control humanity.

Demon spirits are negative energies spread to the brain that eventually penetrate the entire body. In most cases, they are summoned by a witch practitioner (usually female), a male warlock, or witch doctor. Demon spirits are very disorderly and destructive; inflicting pain is their aim. Fear motivates evil spirits to continue haunting a person. On the other hand, using the Word of God in all cases causes them to flee in Jesus's name. More than likely, most of these magic remedies have a cause and effect to some degree.

Multitudes cast spells of magic for different reasons. Spell magic happens as a daily ritual for many to improve their quality of life. Contagious magic is another formula magical practitioners use to affect their target as desired. Contagious magic passes from one person to another either by direct contact with the person or by indirect contact, such as contact with his or her clothes or other personal items. Contagious and Sympathetic magic both share the belief that one thing or event can affect another from distance, also known as Voodoo. This can occur between an individual and any part of his/her body so believers take precaution of their hair, fingernails, clothes, teeth, blood and more.

Spell casters are notorious for manipulating and controlling the flow of energy through magic simply by reinforcing change for themselves or others, change for the betterment of the environment, or change to intentionally cause harm.

In modern society, the practice of using magic is an ancient tradition passed down through generations. From my personal experience, the adversary utilizes a substance called negative energy, or black energy. Although it's not visual to the human eye, it can be seen spiritually. The enemy uses negative energy as means to penetrate human anatomy. It's the main culprit for damaging a person's livelihood, mind, and physical body. This is his main source of power and control; it's a spiritual force capable of manipulation throughout the universe. The extent of this manipulation depends on the strength of the attacking negative energy.

Demons and ghosts are fundamentally the same. They're the souls of dead people who don't want to or cannot move on. They want to control people's bodies so they can live through them. Only a small percentage wishes the living harm.

Demons are supposedly invisible spirits. Spirits that sexually harass individuals are likely demon spirits. Demons are also described as evil spirits, devils, familiar spirits, and demonic spirits. Black magic, as well as other forms of magic, is invisible to the eye, leaving no evidence to be seen. It manifests as an unconstructive substance resonating throughout the airwaves, infiltrating the human mind and thoughts in hopes of gaining complete control over the mind. Depending on the amount of negative substance used, possible side effects can be devastating, prohibiting one's ability to think, concentrate, or function. They can create doubt, create fear, cause anger, cause mental behavior problems, insanity, suicidal tendencies, and confusion. The list keeps going.

One of the major effects of the enemy is to use negative energy to cause reactions in the physical body. The mind and head are the first to be attacked, leading to headaches either on one side or both, blurred vision, and irrational emotional thinking, to name a few. Ultimately, unpleasant scenes lying dormant, waiting for the perfect opportunity to present themselves. Then suddenly, we're taken utterly by surprise.

MANIPULATION OF ENERGIES

Through the craftiness of human witches, warlocks, and associates, I was seduced by demon spirits through bewitchment. Depending on the motive of a person, energy can either be used to benefit humankind or to cause harm. It must be something that the person had contact with. There's a group of devil worshippers in town, camouflaging their premeditated aggressive behaviors and concealing their devious acts of dissension. They secretly hide behind their prestige as law-abiding, established citizens in the local community and surrounding area. I never suspected a large segment of individuals desired nothing more than to see the day I am executed. These individuals were undeniably dedicated to the operation of evil, failing to recognize they're bringing retribution and condemnation on themselves.

It's a misconception to believe all Christians love God; we can interpret this as false delusions. Honestly, I was very naïve to believe all believers love Christ. Some of them have the appearance of Christians, but their inward hearts are dark. Our physical bodies contain energy. An energy field is defined as a field of energy which surrounds and penetrates the body. The aura underlies and supports the functioning of the body. Every human body, planet, plants, animals, things, and objects have tons of energy. Energy is what makes the world function; without it, there is no life.

Everything in life is a close relative and closely intimate with God's divine energy and power source, such as the sun, the moon, the stars, planets, day and night, human life, work environment, and more. Civilization gets the energy it needs from resources such as fossil fuels, nuclear fuel, or renewable energy. The energy and power operating in the world affects the world's environment.

One's emotional state stems from the energy source as well as brain function, our willpower, circumstances, and energy level. Human existence needs energy for survival and to maintain a functioning life. People use energy in many forms. For instance, energy is like having a battery with tons of current to keep the population operational. Depending on the ways energy is used, there can be an adverse effect or a positive effect. They can range from support to manipulation. A human uses his or her energy field as a form of control manipulation. Many people manipulate energy for malicious reasons instead of using energy to help someone. They would rather use energy to harm. It takes a human more energy to be mad or discontent than to be positive. Negative energy tries to control the emotional part of your mind feeding the mind with self-doubt. According to laws of Attraction our thoughts, feelings, words, and actions produce energies which, in turn, attract like energies. Negative energies attract negative energies and positive energies attract positive energies.

Demons, evil spirits, and ghosts are similar in nature. They are perceived as disembodied spirits of people and animals. Devils, demons, and ghosts are comprised of energies. Magic is defined as pure energy. It is solely the responsibility of a practitioner to decide whether magic will be used for the good of humanity or to cause harm. Magic is the manipulation of energy. I have read many articles about energy. It seems that all matter is energy, and our world is comprised of energy. Some of the world is visible energy, or matter, and some is invisible energy.

If we take this same idea and apply it to life forms, such as human beings, we can see it is possible for us to have a soul. The soul would be invisible energy connected to our visible energy: the body. All life forms—plants and animals—must have an energy core. It is this same "soul energy" that likely comprises ghosts and spirits. The difference is that a ghost, or spirit, is a non-domiciled energy, meaning the soul. Energy is matter, and matter is energy (Angels and Ghosts: Exploring Ghost and Spirit Phenomena).

VICTORY OVER OPPOSITION

In writing manuscript, I have been distracted. From all angles, things have tried to distort my focus. As of 2015, goodness and mercy started showing up to bring new life. I am here to tell the world how God has miraculously delivered me from the deadly attacks of the enemy. Now that my mind is clear, it is obvious everything was well orchestrated, structured, and organized by the witch practitioner and her associates. What she and her associates failed to realize was though they may have plotted my beginning, they didn't know my ending. If the enemy fight against you without a cause and you belong to Christ, the Lord will fight against those who fight against you. The Holy Spirit will guide us through our tribulations as we continue to apply God's word. For every opposition God will provide a way of escape.

God has finally allowed me to release what has been bottled up inside me for so long. God has restored everything the enemy tried to steal from me—my marriage, finances, and family. I have a mission in life, and I walk with purpose and dignity. I don't regret having these unfortunate accounts with unseen forces of darkness manifested in the flesh. What I thought was hopeless and insignificant turned out to be

God's ulterior motive to bring people to salvation. His plans were more highly developed than my tribulations. He used my adversity to show the irreligious individuals that he's acutely aware of the injustice plaguing humanity. There's nothing hidden that won't be unveiled. According to Matthew 10:26–27 (NIV), "There is nothing concealed that will not be disclosed, or hidden that will not be made known. What I tell you in the dark, speak in the daylight; what is whispered in your ear, proclaim from the housetops."

There's no greater love than the Lord Jesus Christ, who's no respecter of person. The presence of God is within reach of me; the coolness of his Spirit takes my breath away. Beautiful is the order of the day. My smiles bring out the best in me. The price of freedom was costly. The reward of being freed is miraculous but not achieved without a struggle. The most surprising aspect of my life is that I am here as a living testimony, alive unto God, and profoundly grateful for his deep compassion toward me. Through much praying, my strength was restored, releasing the hidden power underneath the surface. Triumph doesn't come so easily. I had to fight the good fight of faith (1Timothy 6:12 KJV).

It is true that once your dilemma of torment ends, the past seems irrelevant because God has wiped away the tears. I give the enemies two thumbs-up for giving their every attempt to obliterate my existence. I have been waiting a long time for my unusual circumstances to change. In every attempt while pursuing victory, it was mandatory that I stay persistent without taking my focus off hope. Everyone seems designated to confront spiritual darkness at some point. Apparently, my spiritual darkness came unexpectedly. My spiritual darkness searched me out until finally catching up to me, unaware. I had to stand firm in the face of adversity and depend on the Lord to clear me of all charges against me. I admit ending my life seemed like the right thing to do on many occasions.

I've gained insight into spiritual warfare and the enemy. To stand firm against the enemy, you must not be passive. Be more aggressive, and stand your ground. God's Word must be activated and used as the driving force in our lives to give us sound instructions. Once fear is in motion, the enemy uses your mind and fears to torment us, even if it a simple problem. Even though the enemy uses scare tactics to intimidate God's people, all we need to remember is that he is just a big bully. Remember, the enemy is scared that you represent Christ. He's just a bully, and so are his associates.

Even though evil was in full operation, motivated by spell magic that did not determine the outcome of my situation. I ventured through significant changes over the years, enduring such madness. In many instances, people don't quite understand the magnitude of being under such tremendous pressure, barricaded amid poisonous snakes striking nonstop. More important, intense conditioning deepens depending on the severity and harshness of those strikes that might become a life-threatening situation, needing immediate attention. One's emotional state makes it hard to concentrate, and nothing else matters except ending the agony. The emotional stability of that individual becomes unbalanced, making it unbreakable to cope. The mind, not the heart, attempting to deceive the individual into thinking the situation is hopeless.

I admit the ending was harsher than the beginning; the spiritual attacks increased tremendously. But through much praying, my strength was restored, releasing the hidden power underneath the surface. I was driven by circumstances to confront the stronghold as never before. With God's unwavering love, he rescued me from the evil one's plan to destroy my life. My experience taught me many human devils are working undercover for the lord of evil.

My life was liberated through nonstop perseverance, and I continue to be steadfast in my belief in God. I pleaded before the Lord to consider the evidence and justify me in the presence of my enemies. The best defense attorney is the Lord God Almighty, who's able to vindicate, exonerate, and validate any person wrongly accused. I suffered in silence because no one could hear my heartfelt cries. It's breathtaking to recognize my most deeply rooted, weighed-down stumbling block has finally lifted.

My grandchildren used to have disturbing dreams of something dreadful happening to us, especially to me. Without hesitating, it was my duty to reassure the children God wouldn't allow anything to hurt us. Parents often overlook their children instead of listening to them; we brush the child off. But God gives warnings and caution through children's dreams, so pay close attention. They might be saving your life. I've always listened to my grandchildren's dreams because there is something significant about a dream. If their thoughts are important to them, listen.

In my case, every dream my grandchildren had did, in fact, occur. Not only that, but they witnessed many disturbing events. During those dark moments, God gave them dreams relating to my situation. Throughout my ordeal, however, I was unable to dream. Now I've started to dream again, little by little.

It's no secret the enemy of God constantly attempts to annihilate our minds and thought processes through demonic activity. I had moments when my emotions were in high gear that I worked hard not to offend anyone or blurt out insulting words. I was losing my sense of reality, my self-identity, and self-esteem, watching it gradually fades away. No one had any answers, but their encouraging words provided me with the motivation to keep fighting, using the Word of God. I was convinced to never give up and to have faith that God would bring me through. My bishop always mentioned it was more with me than with them (the angels).

I was tormented by wickedness in the worst way imaginable, triggering severe distress and opposition. In an unsubtle way, spiritual darkness searched me out until finally catching up to me. I asked God not to let them tear my soul to pieces for their hearts were evil and wicked day and night. Unless someone experiences a similar situation, they will never understand your opposition.

My faith was challenged daily to the point of exhaustion. Yet quitting wasn't an option. Temptation tried luring me into its deadly snare of entrapment, enticing me to sin. Temptation doesn't present itself as something new but, rather, something you're already familiar with. Temptation's duty is to present opportunities for enticement. Sin is the worst invention known to humankind. If individuals are not careful, thoughts can ensnare their actions without considering the consequences. Subsequently, your flesh reasons with the body as to why you should fulfill your desire. Now your mind contemplates whether to pursue your ambition.

Everything is glamorized, making it appear to all your senses as good. This is where we give the enemy free range to enter our lives. When things are out of balance in your life, you tend to seek comfort in some other form. The adversary's evil agenda starts by identifying a susceptible person to entice by temptation, lowering his or her standards to commit sin. The person commits sins against themselves, family, marriages, and against what is morally right. Now the enemy and his minions have ammunition to use against the person who sinned for his gain, possibly threatening your future. He's laughing in his kingdom because he is doing what he does best—breaking down the family unit and isolating people.

My attitude wasn't always pleasant. My anguish raged deeply hidden beneath the surface. I had to express with deepest sincerity what was bothering me without exploding. I was agitated and miserable, and unable to cope. Reality seemed distant, and my world was tinted with evil. Confusion caused me to be hypothetical, moody, incoherent, and complicated at times. The spirits were becoming stronger and aggressively inflicted me with severe pressure. I was tired of talking in repetition, repeating the same thing over and over. I released my frustration by lashing out at my family members. I would have been weak if I didn't let out frustration. Don't ever think negative spirits can't influence your speech or actions. It happens to the best of us, even if we don't acknowledge it. My marriage was bound for destruction. Unnecessary disputes constantly erupted, building roadblocks between us. I knew our marriage was targeted, causing unnecessary tension and strife. The enemies go to great links to deceive individuals into thinking spiritual darkness doesn't exist.

The objective of the perpetrators was to successfully eradicate everything meaningful—my marriage, children, grandchildren, loved ones, and friends—leaving me with nothing. It wasn't enough to obliterate me alone. God turned everything that was supposed to be destroyed into something far greater. God honors the prayers of the righteous. The Holy Ghost is an important person close to my heart. He never left me to fend for myself. Rather, he comforted me, speaking to me, protecting me from every snare and entrapment, and reassuring me of God's love and promises. To take it even further, in a renowned, soft-spoken voice, I was prompted by the Holy Ghost to inform my bishop of my circumstances, and everything would surely end. Guess what? It happened!

I dared not show my true identity as this was illegal. I wore the faces of many smiles, counteracting those hidden mysteries of despair. The piercing evidence on my face filled with emotion would be noticeable, possibly undressing my secret agenda.

Living in a strange land with so much corruption and evilness would be impossible to survive. When the evil forces are coming against you, just know God and his angelic hosts are working to free you. To combat the enemy hostility aimed against you. Never avenge yourselves. Leave it to the wrath of God, for it is written, "Vengeance is mine, I will repay, says the Lord" (Romans 12:19).

The immorality and malice that was the scourge over my life is finally over. It's high time for a new chapter of contentment and peace. I had plenty of opportunities to think back to the onslaught of these iniquitous events many times. I used to blame myself for the insensitive mistreatment by others. Basically, those rebellious individuals tried to prevent me from enjoying life. Demon-possessed individuals are under the heavy control of demonic influences. They were undeniably dedicated to their initial operation of evil. But what they failed to recognize was that they were bringing retribution and condemnation on themselves. Through manipulation, bewitchment was there to accomplish their twisted ambitions. In essence, they wanted complete control. My enemies were cowardly and immature. It was obvious who was operating behind the scenes besides the adversary. I was hunted down like a most wanted criminal, and the foes paid out plenty of money to catch me. I was spied on, no matter my location. If I wasn't disfigured or damaged enough, they increased my suffering. I wondered if they thought their spell magic wasn't working.

No matter how many objects are buried in my yard, God still holds the keys to my future. Going through the storms brought positive changes in my life. I focus more on being positive than on being negative. Besides, negativism is a red flag in most cases. This was definitely a nightmare that tormented me to the core. This wasn't my cup of tea. The enemy has no color preference when it comes to devouring your soul.

My prayer is that everyone learns to pray and intercede for each other despite our differences, because your adversary, the devil, lies in waiting, like a roaring lion, looking for someone to dismantle. I can't explain everything that happened because I believe it is inappropriate and too graphic and horrifying. But I included the necessary details I thought were appropriate for this writing.

INSIGHT INTO DEMONIC OPPRESSION AND POSSESSION

Money and profit speak volumes to business establishments across the world. The sole purpose of companies is to make a profit in exchange for products, goods, and services. There are millions of merchants selling magical products for financial gain. Those looking for magical products can find just about any magic, herbs, spells, curses, potions, hexes, conjures, books, prayers, blessings, healings, and more. They are no different from any other company. Magic is big business, and it's legal in the United States, but not in some other countries. The problem I have with merchants who sell magic products is that they know customers could be purchasing these items to harm others.

It's easier than ever to buy products online, and magic products are no exception. For the right price, magic practitioners can conjure up the perfect formula to satisfy paying customers. A customer has the option of choosing spells or potions to best suit their particular situations. The enemy glorifies everything harmful, making it seem that there aren't any repercussions or consequences behind it. Read your Bible.

Witchcraft magic is known throughout the entire Bible, and it is forbidden by God.

As I wrote earlier, I have researched demon spirits, magic, and other evil spirits. Let's clear some misconceptions as to whether magic can affect people. Yes, based on personal experience, I believe spell magic affects human nature to some degree. Innocent lives across the nation are targeted by the spirits of witchcraft. Nothing is being done, so these vicious cycles continue to plague innocent people. Over time, I became accustomed to evil spirits, so I am no longer frightened by their presence. Demon spirits are fully aware of those who manifest spiritual authority and power to command spirits to leave.

There is a danger of not believing in demon spirits because they are a reality. Many believers and nonbelievers refuse to believe this truth. A person's spirit is protected, but the flesh is not. Therefore, it's possible to have a demon attach itself to a person, even a true born-again believer. If Satan, devil, demon, and evil spirit don't exist, it makes Jesus Christ's teaching invalid.

Demonic oppression and possession share the common interests of pursuing and subduing the person's body. Demonic oppression occurs when a demon influences someone's behavior. They may cause a person to change in different ways. A person's personality, attitude, and manners may be a few things that change. Yet the person will still have control of his or her physical body.

When a demon has full control over a person's body, it's called demonic possession. The person has no control over his or her physical body, will, consciousness, or freedom. The demon uses the body to communicate with other people through a different voice, personality, and actions. Demon spirits are disembodied spirits in need of a human body to attach to in an attempt to oppress or possess the body. A demon enters the body internally and attaches to a body. Evil spirits want to live out their lives as if they still inhabit their own bodies. Once they inhabit a person's body, they can cause the person to have mental, physical, and emotional sickness.

The goal of the evil one is to take control of the mind and everything else relating to you. Many people around the globe suffer in silence due to witchcraft. There is really no justice for sufferers of black magic or satanic magic or any other kind of magic. Victims of any type of magic must have a strong faith in God. They must be persistent in prayer and have a faithful pastor who constantly prays for their deliverance. They can seek professional help if necessary. They can use incense, especially sage, to clear negative spirits. They can do a self-cleansing and look on the Internet about things pertinent to their situations. Perhaps my story might help someone to identify these same or similar conditions. There's no secret that this destructive spell magic is an epidemic throughout the universe. But most people think it's just a figment of your imagination.

There is no denying that witchcraft is a tradition practiced all over the world with different sets of rules and beliefs. Using various methods, witches call on deities and goddesses from whom they gain powers in form of spells, summons, incantations, divinations, charms, and potions.

I have read that magic can be used for good or evil, depending on the intention of the individual. I have also read that if you don't believe in magic, nothing will happen. This is an incorrect statement. Most people think magic is not real when, in fact, the Bible depicts magic as evil. The weapons of the enemy were formed against me, but rather than prospering, he failed miserably. I always tell individuals just because you haven't seen something take place doesn't necessarily mean it didn't happen. No one can criticize you for what you have experienced and seen in this life. Spiritual darkness has no special preference for their next target. Apparently darkness strikes without warning.

There are many reasons a person might become possessed. As mentioned previously, these include rebelliousness, having a reprobated mind, or a willingness to use your soul as a down payment for material gain. This is why it doesn't pay to use controlled and illegal substances obsessively. Use could lead to either spiritual dependence or spiritual addiction. Spiritually speaking, these substances draw spirits to keep you in bondage.

The word "witchcraft" is a spiritual essence, just like any other word in the dictionary. It's the motive behind witchcraft that makes it unpresentable, especially if it is intended to harm.

Spiritual witchcraft is associated with various forms of magic. Black magic consists of rituals primarily used to harm another person. It can range from making them fall in love to vengeful spells without their permission to them being injured or even killed. Spiritual witchcraft's objective is to attack the mind, including your imagination. It's not good to give in to your imagination because the enemy does everything to make it a reality. The enemy feeds off your fear, using it to terrorize you and to gain complete control over your mind. Jesus Christ has all the power; Satan has limited power here on Earth.

The enemy is crafty, and his aim is to sabotage your life by any means necessary. Bear in mind the enemy doesn't care for anyone. Many true believers love God and attend church faithfully, but the fact remains that you can become affected by spell magic. Even if a person doesn't necessarily believe in spell magic, it doesn't mean it won't take effect. Christ is my life, but even so, evil present through the working of spell magic affected me against my will. Many weapons of the adversary may form against you; it doesn't have to overtake you. Isaiah 54:17 said, "No weapon that is formed against thee shall prosper; and every tongue that shall rise against thee in judgment thou shalt condemn. This is the heritage of the servants of the Lord, and their righteousness is of me, saith the Lord." The difference is a true believer can't be overtaken by enemy attacks except for choosing to give up the battle instead of being persistent despite opposition.

There are numerous websites that practice the art of magic.

The Internet provides easy access to go even further and find practically any spell desired. Movie makers in Hollywood have created movies centered on angels both good and bad, ghosts, black energy, demons, imps, and yes, even evil spirits therefore it's not imaginary. Magic is used in many cultures for healing, keeping away evil, seeking the truth, and for vengeful purposes.

Demon spirits are negative energy (black energy) substances that spread to the brain and eventually penetrating the entire body. From my experience, negative energy is the adversary's main source of power and control, capable of manipulating any process on the earthly plane. Society isn't aware of this negative energy so we fall prey to its effects. In our mind, we think that if we can't see what is happening then it's not really there, but if we can see it, and then it's real. Not everyone is gifted to be able to sense this energy, but it's there. The extent of this manipulation depends on the strength of the attacking negative energy.

Ghosts transmit their black energy to the people they target/attack and create large stores of it in their bodies. The only way to relieve black energy is through a generalized spiritual remedy, such as a spiritual practice or a more specific one like the saltwater treatment (spiritual science research foundation http://www.spiritualresearchfoundation.org/spiritual-healing/self-healing/salt-water-remedy/).

As discussed earlier, depending on the amount of negative substance used, serious side effects can be devastating, even leading to insanity and suicidal tendencies. One can also experience debilitating headaches and blurred vision.

There's salvation, protection, redemption, power, faith, love, and happiness in the blood of our Lord through Jesus Christ. Life is supposed to construct itself precisely as a means of building a firm foundation. Ultimately, unpleasant scenes lie dormant, waiting for the perfect opportunity to present themselves. A believer, the enemy is truly no threat to us. Since God is for his true believers, who can be against the God who dwells in you?

FORGIVING YOUR ENEMIES

Without hesitation, it's better to forgive than not to forgive. I've seen evil take its best effort against me. Undoubtedly, every wrongful act was prearranged. I have witnessed each perpetrator blinded by selfish intent conduct ill-will malice day by day.

I forgave my enemies a long time ago. Not only that, but I chose to love them. I have various reasons not to forgive, but it was a commission by God to forgive. Now I have no hate in my heart. It was an act of my faith to forgive. Forgiveness is mandatory. As long as you harbor unforgiveness, the harder it is to forgive. Forgiveness, in general, is for you or me to move beyond our circumstances and let go of discord. If you take the Bible at face value, then Christ instructed us to forgive. There's no if (Matthew 6:14–15).

Those who were subjective against my forgiveness stretched far beyond their devious ways, and I didn't think twice about forgiving them. It takes an uneducated fool to purposely transgress against someone, but it takes the purest of heart to forgive and love fools unconditionally. Forgiveness is evil's worst enemy because if you don't forgive, you give the enemy an advantage to continue to harbor hatred in your heart. Forgiving someone's offenses is not so easily done; you must practice forgiveness. I don't hate the witches, warlocks, predators, and their associates. They were under the control and influence of the evil one, to inadvertently carry out his wicked scheme. All is not lost.

God desires for us to forgive those who trespass against us. According to Mathew 6:14–15, the Lord commands us to forgive men their trespasses and your heavenly Father will also forgive you. But if you do not forgive those who trespass against you, neither will your Father forgive yours. It's not easy to forgive someone's offenses. Individuals often harbor unforgiveness in their hearts, unwilling to let go of past animosities.

Only until you truly forgive will you be free from bondage. Indeed, learning to forgive is to love unconditionally. Without true forgiveness, there is no peace. People hold grudges toward each other rather than forgive each other. God loaned us family, so let's treasure the family, no matter what. No one is perfect, so learn to forgive and let pride go. Pride keeps us from attaining many good things in life.

We all have the same Spirit as God; we are created entirely in his image. Why is there so much fighting and backbiting against each other? The enemy gets away with assassinations, enjoying the comfort of your misery. If we only knew who's pulling all the strings, we'd resist the enemy's devious scheme. "Our Father, who art in heaven, hallowed be Thy name, Thy kingdom come, Thy will be done on earth as it is in heaven. Give us this day our daily bread; and forgive us our trespasses as we forgive those who trespass against us; and lead us not into temptation, but deliver us from evil. For thine is the kingdom and the power and the glory forever and ever. Amen" (Psalm 23:1).

Thanks to these ungodly individuals under the enemy's control, I have gained more insight on the kingdom of God and the kingdom of Satan. The weapons of the enemy were formed against me but failed miserably. If you know someone who has committed a transgression, and you're totally aware of his or her intention, you are guilty by association.

BIBLE SCRIPTURES

The one True God: John 17:3; Jeremiah 10:10; 24:7; Psalm 115

Only God: 1 Corinthians 8:4, 6; 1 Timothy 2:5; Romans 3:30; James 2:19; Revelation 1:8; Mark 12:29, 32; Isaiah 43:10, 11; 44:6; Deuteronomy 6:4; John 10:30; Ephesians 4:6; Malachi 2:10

God is distinctive: Joshua 1:8; Psalm 19:7–11, Psalm 119:105, 160; Isaiah 40:7–8; 2 Timothy 3:16–17; 4:3; Hebrews 4:12; 1 Peter 1:22–2:2; 2 Peter 1:20–21

No other God besides him: Deuteronomy 4:35; 32:39; Psalm 18:31; Isaiah 43:10; 45:5

God is intimate with creation: Genesis 1; 2; Isaiah 40:12–15; 44:24; John 1:1–5; Romans 11:33–36; 1 Thessalonians 4:3–5; Matthew 10:30

The eternal God: Genesis 21; 33; Psalm 90:2; 93:2; Isaiah 9:2; 57:15; Habakkuk 1:12; 1 Timothy 1:17; Revelation 1:8

Intimate God: John 3:16; Psalm 42:1–2; 51:1–19; 63:1–11;

139:1–24; 1 Corinthians 6:13; 2 Peter 1:3; Revelation 22:12–14; Joshua 1:9; Proverbs 2:1–11

God is both transcendent and immanent: Isaiah 40:22; 54:5; 55:9; Psalm 113:5–6; Deuteronomy 4:7; Ezekiel 34:11, 15

God is Spirit: Genesis 1:2; 6:3; 41:38; Exodus 31:3; Numbers 27:18; 35:31; Nehemiah 9:20; Job 32:8; 33:4; Psalm 139:7; Isaiah 11:2; 32:15; 40:13; 42:1; 44:3–4; 48:16; 51:12; 59:19–21; 61:1; 63:14; Ezekiel 11:24; 36:27; 37:9, 14, 39:29; Haggai 2:5; Zechariah 4:1–7; 12:10; Joel 2:28–29; Micah 2; 3:8; 2 Chronicles 15:1; 24:20; 1 Samuel 10:10; 19:20; Matthew 3:16; 1 Corinthians 2:11–14; 2 Corinthians 3:3; Philippians 3:3; 1 Peter 4:14; John 4:4; 4:21–24

Demonic possession in the Bible: Matthew 9:32–33; 12:22; Mark 5:1–20; 7:26–30; Luke 4:33–36; 22:3; Acts 16:16–18

Simulacrum Doll
Known as the "Voodoo Doll"

A Person doesn't necessarily have to be a witch or warlock to be involved in the occult to practice magic. The voodoo doll is described as a doll in which pins and needle are inserted. The voodoo doll is simply a simulacrum. A simulacrum, effigy or poppet doll is an object that is the likeness of an individual or object. So the voodoo doll is a likeness of a person and is used to represent that person. Once psychic connection is made between the voodoo doll and that person, whatever you do to the doll affects the person. Although it comes in various different forms, such practices are found in the magical traditions of many cultures across the world. There are many types of voodoo dolls for all purposes, such as love, healing, career, empowerment, fame, guidance, fertility or cursing. Many people around the globe have learned how to use voodoo dolls for many types of rituals. Depending on the purpose and practices of using a voodoo doll, it can benefit the environment or harm someone. An individual may use a voodoo doll as a way to improve their situation. Such as in healing an ailments, finding employment, finding love, improving life circumstances, financial prosperity, as well as a continuous list of things. A voodoo doll can cause harm to an individual without their consent. This is where I come in; a voodoo doll was used against me. The thoughts of pins and needles penetrating my entire physical body were torture. Using the simulacrum doll was another form of control to impose physical abuse from head to toe. Because the evil one represents hell and hell represents heat, fire, and pain; the evil one would constantly sends waves of heat throughout my body. I experience an unusual crawling sensation, headache, itching, twitching, blurred vision, as well as stinging throughout my entire body. The only thing that gave me relief was prayer as well as other methods. Remember individuals who perform such operations are under the influence of evil spirits in motion. Although they used seductive spell magic controlling me wasn't as easy as they thought. The only way this is done is through a personal item of someone. A witch practitioner gathers personal belongings from the individual along with other objects and places them inside a container to be buried nearby. No two people are alike and individuals causing intentional harm against someone must have the correct objects of that person in order for their spell to be executed correctly. We are made of energy; the clothes we wear have energy, your picture, nails, hair, etc. They barely use material items of a person because it has no value; it has to be something with your energy. But this can only be operated through the control of the evil one. Where does the power come from? No objects of any kind have any power except what evil offers. Voodoo dolls work because they focus the energy of multiple spells into a single item. Therefore, when you order a Voodoo doll you are not just getting a doll - you are getting multiple spells infused into a material object crafted especially to be a magical home for those spells.

Definition and Meaning

Neither magic spell nor curse has any supernatural power except for to be summoned by the evil one for harmful purposes.

Curse is also known as imprecation. Curse is referred as the expression of a wish that misfortune, evil, doom, causing harm to another etc. Using a negative word toward self or someone can be considered a curse.

Magic is considered as having powers to influence the course of events by using mysterious or supernatural forces. Magic is used by many people for varieties of reason to gain a specific outcome. Magic has no color preference; magic is all about your energy, your intentions.

Magicians perform tricks, magic shows, illusionists, card tricks, staged performances.

Magick refer to actual spells such as love, protection, even curse. Magik is used to differentiate between those who pretend to have powers and those who seek to learn about the unseen powers and forces of nature.

Warlock refers to a male practitioner who practices magic or sorcery.

Wizard refers to person who practices magic; magician, sorcerer, conjurer or juggler.

Sorcerer refers to (paranormal), a practitioner of magic, the ability to attain objectives or acquire knowledge or wisdom using supernatural means Sorcerer (fantasy), someone who uses or practices magic that derives from the supernatural.

Voodoo Doll is commonly employed to describe an effigy into which pins are inserted. Although a magic doll comes in various different forms, such practices are found in the magical traditions of many cultures across the world. A candle is an ignitable wick embedded in wax, or another flammable solid substance such as tallow, that provides light, and in some cases, a fragrance.

A **candle** can also provide heat, or be used as a method of keeping time. Like any other magic, candles have a closely related connection with magic. Candles come in varieties of scented and assorted colors. Candles can be use to gain prosperity, reverse a spell, love, gain employment, etc. Colors candle have different symbolic meaning.

A **hex** refers as bewitch; practice witchcraft on someone or something. A hex can have harmful or protective intentions.

A **Charm** is a kind of jewelry or object to be worn or carry. More so a charm is a power if pleasing or attracting, as through personality or beauty.

White magic can broadly be defined as any kind of magic that is not used malevolently and white magic spells have no malevolent connotations behind them.

Black magic is characterized as gaining supernatural powers in an attempt to cause harm for selfish desires.

Gray magic also known as neutral magic, is a type of magic not completely focused on hostility or being beneficial it's more of a mix between black and white magic.

A **jinn** refers to as spirits, lower than the angels, capable of appearing in human and animal forms and influencing humankind for either good or evil.

Contagious magic meaning, magic that attempts to affect a person through something once connected with him or her, as a shirt once worn by the person or a footprint left in the sand; a branch of sympathetic magic based on the belief that things once in contact are in some way permanently so, however separated physically they may subsequently become.

Sympathetic magic also known as Imitative Magic., is define as magic predicated on the belief that one thing or event can affect another at a distance as a consequence of a sympathetic connection between them. It's said sympathetic magic is the belief that 'like produces like.' Simply put, what is done to something will cause on outcome on something else. Candle Magic is greatly desired by Witches. Almost always used in magick making, candles are associated with the fire element to bring change.

AUTHOR'S BIOGRAPHY

From childhood to adulthood, God always miraculously intervened in her life. She is truly a living testimony of the goodness of God's supernatural miracles present today. The oldest of four, she was born and raised by her mother in Miami, Florida, until age twenty-four. She graduated from Miami Palmetto Senior High School and earned a certificate as a nursing assistant from South Dade Skill Center. Before she married, she gave birth to a beautiful baby girl at age eighteen. Married at age twenty-four, as a military spouse, she relocated with her husband to Denver and then to Las Vegas for thirteen years. She is loved by her husband for thirty-one years. She is the devoted mother of three adult children and grandmother of seven. She earned her associate of applied technology degree in early childhood care and education paraprofessional. She earned a bachelor of science in business management of information technology systems from Kaplan University.

She's continually gravitating toward newer ways of gaining insight, knowledge, and understanding through education, reading, research, and studying. Her life as she imagined it to be should have been full of happiness, but it suddenly changed without warning. Her main agenda is to excel beyond limitations while maintaining a positive outlook on life. She is an ordained minister of the gospel, declaring God's Word to those who have a listening ear. She believes no matter how fierce the wind blows, always maintain faith in God, and stay persistent in praying, having belief in God, and having love for each other.

www.ingramcontent.com/pod-product-compliance
Lightning Source LLC
Chambersburg PA
CBHW060404080526
44583CB00012B/461